MW00717495

BUSINESS RISK ASSESSMENT

By
David McNamee,
CIA, CISA, CFE, CGFM, FIIA(M)

The Institute of Internal Auditors

Disclosure

Copyright © 1998 by The Institute of Internal Auditors, 249 Maitland Avenue, Altamonte Springs, Florida 32701-4201. All rights reserved. Printed in the United States of America. No part of this publication may be reproduced, stored in a retrieval system, or transmitted in any form by any means — electronic, mechanical, photocopying, recording, or otherwise — without prior written permission of the publisher.

The IIA publishes this document for informational and educational purposes. This document is intended to provide information, but is not a substitute for legal or accounting advice. The IIA does not provide such advice and makes no warranty as to any legal or accounting results through its publication of this document. When legal or accounting issues arise, professional assistance should be sought and retained.

ISBN 0-89413-422-1
98239 10/98
99140 8/99

CONTENTS

ABOUT THE AUTHOR

David McNamee, CIA, CISA, CFE, CGFM, FIIA(M), is President of Management Control Concepts, a consulting firm he founded in 1991 to specialize in improving governance processes through improved risk management and internal audit practice. Management Control Concepts serves a worldwide client list from all segments of public and private enterprise.

Prior to forming his own practice in 1991, McNamee was Director - Internal Auditing at Pacific Bell. The balance of his 22-year career at Pacific was spent in Information Systems Project Development and Information Systems line management. He has over 25 years' experience in designing, building, managing, and auditing major systems, including hands-on experience in state-of-the-art business risk assessment for both public and private sector organizations.

McNamee holds a Master of Business Administration as well as a Master of Science in Telecommunications Management. He is a Certified Internal Auditor, Certified Information Systems Auditor, a Certified Fraud Examiner, and a Certified Government Financial Manager. He is the author of The Institute of Internal Auditors (IIA) seminar *Assessing Risk: A Better Way to Audit* and the recent IIA text *Assessing Risk.* He has published additional books, numerous articles, and a "Best Practices" video through The IIA. His articles on risk, fraud, and internal auditing have been published in the United States, Europe, Asia, and the South Pacific. He is a frequently invited speaker at major internal audit conferences on six continents, and he has given seminars on risk in more than 12 countries.

McNamee's other major honors include the Ratliff Award for service to The IIA (New Zealand). He is also the only overseas Fellow elected by The IIA (Malaysia). He is currently Chairman of The IIA international Relations Committee and a member of the Board of Directors of IIA, Inc. In addition to his IIA activities, he is a member of the Association of Certified Fraud Examiners, the Association of Government Accountants, and the Institute of Management Consultants.

CHAPTER 1
THE NATURE OF CHANGE

Organizations exist in a constantly changing environment. Understanding the nature of change is important to understanding the changing environment as the source of risk to the organization.

Organizations are in the midst of change. They are in the turbulent transition between the industrial age and the information age. Our technology has changed quite a lot, but many of our organizations have not. The stress this creates is evidenced by the massive restructuring of the industrialized countries as both business and government downsize, reengineer, and reinvent themselves.

Technology has spread information widely, and information has become a source of empowerment. Frontline people often know what is going on with customers of the organization long before the chief executive, yet the hierarchical structure of most organizations stifles the ability to act quickly on that information. But frontline people are hampered by a restricted view. The central core of the organization, with a wider view of the interaction of the environment on the organization, must take the lead in dealing with change through strategic leadership.

Strategic planning in organizations seems to go in and out of style, probably because the plans are drawn up in a vacuum without a good real-world understanding of the nature of change. Strategic thinking and strategic leadership are always in style. Leading by imagination and vision enables the organization to "peer around the corner" at change that no one else can see. Managers need to engage in strategic thinking so they can deal with impending threats or take advantage of upcoming opportunities.

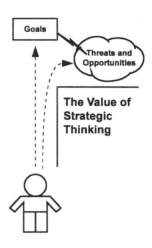

The Value of Strategic Thinking

By examining the patterns of change and interpreting their meaning, it is possible to anticipate certain types of environments. This interpretation forms the basis for our thinking models that are used to predict where these changes are leading the organization. Only then can the strategists deal with the uncertainties and risks in the universe.

Change is not an event — it is a process of living and growing in the environment. Systems in nature are full of success stories of organisms that changed and adapted to their environment. Those organisms that stayed connected to their environment thrived, changing as the environment changed. Those organisms that did not stay connected failed to adapt, and they died.

Organizations are social structures that act in many ways like organisms. The environment of organizations includes customers, government regulation, competition, and technology. Those organizations that can stay connected to important changes in their environment will succeed. Others will cease to exist. The Fortune 500 is a lot different today than it was 20 years ago because the same process of "adapt-or-die" is at work.

Adaptation to the environment happens in a natural cycle. The cycle of adaptation does not come around in a circle or loop, because the environment is changing, too. The growth pattern is more like a spiral upward toward more complexity and more functionality to whatever ultimate existence there is. Flatten out that spiral for two-dimensional graphics and it is a series of interlocking "S" curves. Each "S" curve represents a complete cycle, and each cycle can be studied as a series of three phases, with a critical boundary between each phase where adaptation and transformation take place. It is at these points that the organism or organization becomes something else entirely — related to the past, but not a simple extension of it.

To approach the study of business risk, we need to understand the cycle of change. What we mean by change is not just incremental improvement, nor is change a radical new invention with little or no foundation in the past. Both theories have proponents, but neither of these two concepts are adequate models for change.

Our model for understanding the cycle of change is based in the natural laws of systems and how they adapt to changes in the environment. In his 1973 work, *Grow or Die: The Unifying Principle of Transformation*, Dr. George Land first advanced a model based on natural systems. He later expanded the model with further research into what is known now as the Transformation Theory of systems. Unlike the incremental approach, Transformation Theory explains both the process of change as well as the crucial points when change is not a linear extension of the past. Transformation Theory explains how all systems (physical and social) grow and change.

Systems are collections of parts, functions, or attributes that function together for a common purpose. The systems that concern us con-

tain both people and processes. Systems grow through the dynamic process of change. Since nature has been changing for 4.5 billion years, natural systems provide a rich set of examples for how dynamic change takes place. We can detect three distinct phases of growth in any system, whether that system is social or physical.

Nature abounds with examples of the three stages of growth and transformation. An amethyst in its natural state shows a layer of base rock matrix that is unformed and irregular. Out of this layer grows a pure white quartz with regular rhomboid patterns forming perfect crystals. At some point in the growth of the quartz crystal, a new mineral was introduced, and the quartz was colored purple by the inclusion of something new and different from the outside. The rhomboid shape remains, but the crystal is now a semi-precious amethyst. Each of these three growth periods (rock, quartz, amethyst) is well defined and continuous. At the boundaries between them, however, the rules of change themselves change, and the change is rapid and discontinuous.

One common notion is that *change is linear* (if we know the past of a system we can predict the future). Another belief is that *change is circular* (what has happened once will come around again). Neither of these approaches has

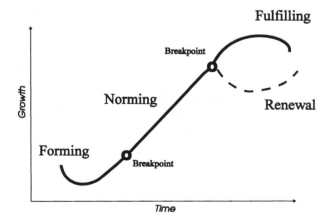

proven a good predictor. There are periods of linear incremental change, and then there are periods of rapid discontinuous change. Our model has three distinct phases of change separated by periods of turbulence and discontinuity. We call these three phases forming, norming, and fulfilling. The periods that separate these phases we call "breakpoints."

It is the same for organizations. The early formative period is characterized by "two steps forward and one step back." Resources may be consumed at an alarming rate, causing the total value of the organization to drop (a downward slope) before there is any success. As the organization grows in learning, the downward slope begins to creep upward. Organizations that do not learn, or are undercapitalized, never make it this far — they are the equivalent of nature's "experiments." If the formative organization connects with its environment (the marketplace, customers/constituents), there is a rapid change in direction. Rather than experimenting and learning, the organization begins to replicate its newfound formula for success as rapidly as possible. This change in operations, from experimenting and learning to replicating and controlling, is the first "breakpoint" where the rules of growth and change themselves change. The rules for this first forming phase? Invent! Create! Try!

A period of linear growth ensues, fueled by improvements on the basic success at the first breakpoint. The growth is focused and controlled by rules of what constitutes success and what does not. Conforming to a normative pattern is valued more than experimenting with new ways. The second phase of growth is equally important for what it *rejects*. This is when the system decides what it will and will not do. It builds barriers to anything that is different from the pattern it has selected. This is how a business maintains its focus. Controls are built upon controls so that all is focused on "what made us great." The organization must form regular, repeatable bonds with the marketplace and strengthen the connection that worked. The rules have changed in this second "norming" phase: Repeat! Improve! Control!

One day the organization is faced with the dilemma of declining results. What worked before no longer works. The environment was changing all along, and the rule-bound organization of the late normative period cannot see that customers' needs had changed or new technology was available to others. A second breakpoint has been reached. Declining output sets the organization in motion to try to extend the linear growth curve. Two methods are usually employed:

1. The "Back to Basics Bump" where the organization pours its entire reserves into "what made us great" before. The result is usually a sharp linear growth spurt followed by complete (or near-complete) disaster. The Battle of the Bulge is one historic example. The supernova is another example from nature.

2. The organization reaches out to incorporate something new and different to make their product/service more valuable. This can change the rate of decline for some time. It can also cause the organization to "jump the curve" to form another organization from the first. At the same time as the second breakpoint is reached, there are others at work to produce something new and different from what went before — using the same purpose, but achieving results in a novel way. The business begins listening to its customers and employees. The business creates a new emphasis on quality and marketing. The business now *has become far more valuable by incorporating the new and different* into its core structures. The rules for this third fulfilling phase of growth: Innovation! Quality! Ideas!

Occasionally, the organization waits too long to find this seed growing within (or smothers it to death). Then the more radical shift is to reengineer, which is a leap from the top of one curve to (hopefully) land on the upward growth curve of the next generation. IBM's switch to the AS/400 is a successful transition. Their personal computer venture is another version. The purchase of Rolm, and later Lotus, is more like trying to incorporate new and different ideas from the outside.

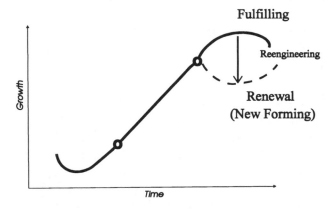

When a successful system makes it over the second breakpoint into phase three, two events happen: it begins to innovate and make improvements in quality rather than quantity, and *simultaneously* it begins to reinvent itself. Invisibly at first, a new cycle of growth begins. Unfortunately, many businesses do not value the chaos that comes with this renewal, because this phase is as jumbled as the original phase one. Mature organizations have a harder time getting back in touch with an environment that has changed and moved on. Ignoring the value of renewal stems from a limited vision and a limited understanding of the purpose of the organization.

Reinvention, if not ignored, becomes first an irritant, then a threat to the parent system, because it will supplant the parent if given enough time. To thrive, the offspring has to be separated from the parent system that gave it birth. Otherwise it can be overwhelmed by the inertia of the old system.

The current form of business was invented nearly 100 years ago and perfected by the likes of Ford, Sloan (General Motors), Vail & Bell (AT&T), and Watson (IBM) to name a few. Western business is now in the latter stages of second phase normalizing growth, where the stresses and strains of systems drifting away from their environment are not readily noticed. Some are even "over the hill" in terms of having peaked some time ago. These are the organizations that reengineer with their backs to the wall.

The nature of change and our model of change make these points evident:

- The uncertain environment does not change or evolve in a straight line.
- There are many "environments" — each of which is changing. This complicates the issue so that precise prediction is nearly impossible.
- By knowing the path of change (the change model) and the characteristics of the three phases of change, it is easier to predict the path the organization will take.
- The most significant risk to an organization is losing touch with its environment.

CHAPTER 2
THE NATURE OF RISK

Q. What is risk analysis?

A. *It is a decision-making tool for considering the* **consequences of alternatives***.*

Q. Why would anyone need to know anything about risk analysis?

A. *Because people make decisions every day about what to accomplish, how much time/resources to spend on the project, and what is important enough to report to the organization.*

Risk analysis includes risk assessment and risk management. These are different phases of making decisions based on risk. Risk assessment is a method of identifying and measuring risk. Risk management is taking action to minimize risk (including installing internal controls):

1. **Risk Assessment:** The quantitative and qualitative evaluation of exposures arising from some activity.
   - Risk identification: The identification and classification of what the risks are and their characteristics.
   - Risk measurement and evaluation: The measurement of possible consequences.
   - Risk prioritization: How the risks are related to each other.

2. **Risk Management:** The process of determining whether or how much of the risk is acceptable and what action should be taken:
   - Diversify or avoid the risk: Changing the nature of the activity to spread the exposure over multiple activities.
   - Sharing the risk: A form of diversification where the parties in the activity take shares of the risk in the activity. Sharing can be with customers, suppliers, or third parties (like insurance).
   - Contingency planning: Establishing controls for known risks.

Generally, management performs both risk assessment (identifying, measuring, and prioritizing) and risk management (doing something about the risk). Risk is based on the "uncertainty principle." This principle means that business decisions are subject to the changes in the business environment due to natural variation (even the best people have a bad day every once in awhile). Risk analysis supports decision analysis. Both are used to incorporate a logical and analytical approach to making decisions and solving problems under uncertain conditions.

Risk analysis and risk assessment are imprecise tools. These tools help us get closer to understanding the problem. The "Basic Law of Decision Analysis" states that a decision system that incorporates uncertainty, even in a flawed way, may well outperform a system that ignores uncertainty. An imprecise tool is better than no tool at all! The corollary to this rule is that we must not expect too much of risk analysis. Risk analysis is only a guide — we still have a lot of work to do after we assess risk.

Exercise: Using Risk Analysis in Decisions

The purpose of this exercise is to demonstrate how managers use risk analysis in decision making and to get participants to think about the nature of risk.

The chief executive needed to make a decision. The headquarters organization had grown and needed more space for operations. There were several alternatives:

1. Purchase the adjacent land parcel and expand the existing facilities.
2. Build an additional facility.
3. Build a new modern building large enough to handle all the extra capacity and then sell the existing older building.
4. Lease additional facilities.

The major uncertainty (and therefore the major source of risk) was in market demand. Headquarters staff size was very market-sensitive. If demand stayed strong, the best long-term, cost-effective decision was to build an entirely new building. If demand faltered or fluctuated widely, then a simple expansion or a short-term lease would be better. The major risk was in market demand, and the CEO commissioned a series of market studies to determine whether the growth was going to be sustained or the market was passing through a fad.

Minor risks also entered into the decision process and risk analysis. Interest rates could have an effect on building versus leasing space. Rumors of a capital investment tax credit could affect the decision to build versus lease facilities. The CEO received advice about the probabilities of these events from the CFO.

The CEO thought about ways to diversify risk in the uncertain market, but could find no way of changing that uncertainty into a certainty. The CEO thought about sharing the risk, and another alternative came to mind: the organization could outsource or subcontract some of the headquarters functions with a company to share the risk of a downturn in the market. There would be higher costs associated with this rather than doing the job in-house, so the opportunity for gain would be smaller than any of the other alternatives.

The CEO also thought about ways to control the known risks. The best plans to control the risk of an uncertain demand was to ensure that the marketing people stayed very close to customers and their needs through major customer visits, customer focus groups and surveys, and funding market research. Interest rate risk could be mitigated through the careful selection of financial instruments, and political risks/opportunities in the tax area would take a back seat to the other issues.

Answer the following questions:

1. Comment on the CEO's thinking process. Who else on the CEO's staff (or others) should provide input? What kind of input could that be?
2. Is there a clear-cut decision to be made? Why or why not?
3. Do you see any additional risks or factors to be considered? Where might we look for additional concerns?

Strategic Risk

Each work unit in the organization puts its assets to work through the management process and internal control system. The work unit objectives are linked to the organization's overall goals and objectives. Risk, in the form of uncertain changes in the environment, can affect the assets and/or the management process. The effects of risk depend also in part on the nature of the assets and the types of management processes and controls.

The primary role of management is to put assets at risk to achieve objectives:

- Human.
- Physical.
- Financial.
- Intangible/informational.

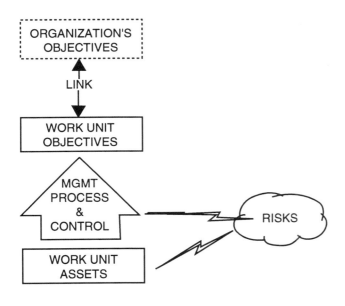

Strategic management sets the plan, organizes the resources, and monitors the result of the organization's conversion of those resources to goods and services for customers or constituents.

Management typically monitors the organization through the internal auditor. The primary role of the internal auditor is to evaluate and

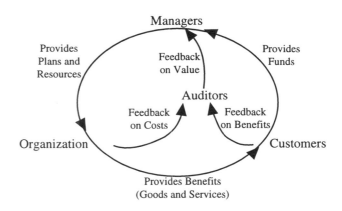

report on management controls which ensure that established objectives for efficiency and effectiveness are met. Resources are efficiently used, and customers' needs are being met. The link between auditors and managers is the assessment of risk and its consequences on achieving established strategic objectives.

Business risk assessment begins with the strategic plans of management and the risks of changing environments. Risk assessment then works downward to the risks in the work units through the chain of supporting unit goals and objectives.

Risk Terms

Risk is a concept. It is a measure of uncertainty (probabilities). In the business process, the uncertainty involves the achievement of organizational objectives. Risk may involve positive or negative consequences, although most positive consequences are known as opportunities, and most negative consequences are called threats or risks.

Consequences are tangible outcomes of risk on the decisions, events, or processes. We cannot see the intangible risk, but we can anticipate and observe the consequences of risk. Risk is neither good nor bad, it just "is." The effects of risk and uncertainty can result in good or bad consequences. When we think of risk, most of us think in terms of consequences rather than pure probabilities.

Consequences can vary in severity depending on a number of factors:

- The assets at risk (our **exposure**).
- The type of threat.
- The duration of the consequence.
- The effectiveness of controls in place.

Exposure is the susceptibility to loss or a perception of a threat to an asset or asset-producing process, usually quantified in dollars. An exposure is the total dollars at risk without regard to the probability of a negative event. Exposure becomes a measure of relative importance when prioritizing audit elements during risk assessment. Generally, the more valuable the asset is to achieving the organization's established objectives, the more important that exposure is to the auditor. Exposure is mitigated by risk management techniques, including building and maintaining effective controls.

Threat is a combination of the risk, the consequence of that risk, and the likelihood that the negative event will take place. Threat is often used in analysis in place of the term "risk." The type of threat is actually an expression of the type of consequence: fire, flood, error, omission, delay, fraud, breakdown, obsolescence, and so forth. Threats come from the operation of risk in the environment, regardless of the controls or control environment. Threats are always present, but controls keep them in check (as long as they are effective).

The **duration of the consequence** affects its severity. As most computer center managers will tell you, if the computer is down for an hour, that's one kind of consequence. If it is down for a day, that's another. If it is down for a week, the organization is likely out of business!

Finally, consequences are affected by the effectiveness of the controls and the internal control system in place. When managers think of risk, they often think in terms of **managed risk**. Managed risk is actually the threats and

consequences *with controls considered.* **Absolute risk** is a term for the threats and consequences without considering the controls likely to be present and operating.

Risk also can be referred to as "High," "Medium," or "Low." Taken literally, that would mean that the probability of occurrence was respectively great, average, or remote. When managers speak of risk in these relative terms (High...Low), they often mean that the consequences of risk are respectively severe, average, or negligible.

The nature of risk and our models for dealing with it make these points evident:

- Risk is a measure of the uncertainty in events or the condition of the environment. What management is focused on are the consequences of the risk.
- The strategic role of management in the organization should be matched with a strategic risk assessment process. The key to the risk assessment process lies in the chain of goals and objectives that permeate the organization.
- Management control systems play an important part in the perception of risk. Strong controls give the impression that risk is minimized, when in fact only the consequences are minimized. There are no practical methods for making uncertain events more certain.
- The management of risk follows the assessment of risk, just like treatment follows diagnosis. To manage risk is the essence of management.

Strategic Influences on Business Risk Assessment

The origins of risk assessment lie in management strategic planning. Strategic planning tries to take into account the long-term view of operations. The longer the view, the more uncertainty that has to be considered.

The old planning adage goes something like this, "When you are up to your armpits in alligators, it is hard to remember that your goal was to drain the swamp." Managers often spend so much time dealing with the significant risks in the present that they find it difficult to deal with risk in a longer time horizon. While we focus on the plans for draining the swamp, the alligators will have us for breakfast! On the other hand, if we do not have some resources devoted to dredging the swamp, the alligators will never go away. How then can we discover the "right" mix of plans over time that will help our organizations achieve their goals?

We have developed a new thinking model for addressing business risk and business opportunity over multiple time horizons. Using this model, organizations have begun to reshape their planning and control systems to be more effective in supporting the organization's goals and objectives.

Structured planning is an effective internal control system. Through planning, managers anticipate the inherent risks in their activities and set up methods to mitigate the effects of these risks. Inherent risks, also known as business risks, exist in all activities. The inherent risk of any activity is a function of the mix of assets and the nature of the activity. For example, a cash teller operation has a degree of business risk within the activity. The assets employed could be:

- Physical assets (building, furnishings, etc.).
- Financial assets (the cash).
- Human assets (teller).
- Intangible assets (policies and procedures, information, etc.).

The biggest inherent risk in a cash teller operation is the loss of the cash asset. We can mitigate some of the business risk by installing security devices (cameras, guards, bandit barriers) and changing the physical asset mix.

Still other business risks could be mitigated by installing an automated teller machine in place of the human teller asset. Management can mitigate other inherent risks by limiting the cash on hand and by installing effective policies and procedures.

What the final asset mix might be in our cash teller operation has a lot to do with which risks we want to mitigate and at what cost. Our overall business objectives are a third factor to consider as well. In our teller example, if we want to make every customer contact a selling opportunity, then the automated teller machine is probably less effective than a human teller/salesperson.

A key concept in our model is that *risk* and *opportunity* are part of a continuum of variation. This is not new: people have associated risk and reward together for some time. However, looking at risk from a systems perspective demonstrates why this is so. Risk is the potential of negative results (less than expected), and opportunity is the potential for positive results (greater than expected). Both are variations from system plans. The results of negative risk are usually not desirable. The results of positive opportunity can be equally undesirable! The fully booked restaurant that must turn away business may never see some of those potential customers again.

The ideal system would mitigate negative risks and take advantage of positive opportunities. Managers that can achieve both control and flexibility are worth their weight in gold.

A second key concept is that the nature of risk and opportunity change over time. In the short term, risk is largely due to system variation: errors, omissions, delays, and fraud prevent us from achieving our goals. These threats loom large to the organization. Opportunity in the short run is small. There is not enough time to exploit fully the opportunities that may exist. The cumulative effect is a strong negative potential outcome.

If we stop our planning at this point, we may erect elaborate and costly control systems to mitigate this short-term negative potential. Many of our internal control systems, growing out of public accounting's focus on current financial statement risk, deal mainly with this short-term negative potential. What is missing from our control systems are ways to deal with mid-term and long-term risk and opportunity.

As we move beyond simple system variation (errors, omissions, delays, and fraud), we have risks that are felt only in future periods. Such risks have to do with resource effectiveness in the mid-term and customer/constituent satisfaction in the longer term. Also we see that different opportunities exist when we consider the effect of time. Resource effectiveness can be improved in the mid-term; however, in the short term we do not have enough time to feel the effects of investment or conservation decisions. In the long term, there are many opportunities with significant payoffs. We could exploit these opportunities if we knew how to take advantage of them.

The effect of time on both risk and opportunity creates a very different scene in each period. In the short run, negative risk overwhelmed anything we could do to take advantage of short-term opportunities. If our planning horizon includes the mid-term values for two or three periods beyond the current accounting cycle, we have greater potential to take advantage of opportunities and more time for plans to mitigate risks to our assets. Instead of being overwhelmed by a negative risk potential, we see the balance as either equal or slightly biased toward the positive opportunities.

In a purchasing system, we can adjust our planning controls and establish programs in the mid-term to seek new sources of supply, to improve our contract administration, and to embark on a program of vendor audits for cost recoveries. The short-term variation risks still exist. We have more time in the mid-term to design controls to deal with risks, so there is a close balance of risk and opportunity in this period.

In the longer term, we have more time to adjust our control system. Negative risk never completely disappears; however, over the long run, the effect of negative variation on the system diminishes considerably with vigilant internal control systems. On the other hand, the number and value of opportunities grow significantly. The positive potential of new markets or new technology overwhelms the negative potential of system variation to create a large positive bias in the long run.

Managers must plan, organize, direct, and control systems to reflect both risk and opportunity. Using our examples of overwhelming negative bias in the short run, equal weighting in the mid-term, and overwhelming positive bias in the long run, we have developed a series of curves.

We have plotted the potential results from the action of risk and opportunity on the organization, both positive and negative, over time. Our model also plots a midpoint between risk and opportunity to reflect the balance needed in the control system to deal effectively with both. This curve of the midpoints we call the Strategic Risk/Opportunity Curve. The Strategic Risk/Opportunity Curve is an effective thinking model to plan control systems to deal with both risk and opportunity over multiple time horizons.

How could we apply this model in a real work situation? Using internal audit as a major control system, how would our understanding of the Strategic Risk/Opportunity Curve affect our decisions?

Internal auditing is a control system that evaluates other control systems. In this role, internal auditing performs a control function for senior management. To fulfill their control role, auditors make two important decisions using risk assessment:

1. What resources to allocate to which business processes (the annual audit plan)?
2. Within each audit, what are the key controls to be evaluated (the individual audit program)?

The natural bias of many internal auditors is to think only of risk to the current business process (short-term variation). With a short-term view, opportunity is rarely examined at all (it is too small in the short term to have any affect). The result will be an audit plan that is heavily weighted to areas of the business with the greatest immediate risk. The auditor usually omits from the annual audit plan or gives short shrift to areas where few assets are at risk, such as planning, product development, and research. Yet it is in these latter areas that the future of the organization will be born — the areas of greatest opportunity.

If internal audit changes their audit plan to give some weight to mid-term and long-term opportunities, they could increase the value of internal audit as a control system. For example, internal audit could test controls that help the organization recognize genuine opportunity from false hope. The auditor also could evaluate funding controls to make sure that management maintains an adequate investment in the future.

At the level of the individual audit, the bias is even stronger. The manager being audited is up to his or her neck in alligators and may not value such mid-term and long-term payoff strategies as investing in new tools and training, planning instead of reacting, or reengineering the business process to meet customer needs more effectively. The internal auditor who uses the thinking model of the Strategic Risk/Opportunity Curve can add steps to the audit program to test for controls that the business unit uses to identify and to take advantage of opportunities or to mitigate system variation over time.

Using a model such as the Strategic Risk/Opportunity Curve will give internal auditors and others a better strategic focus on the relationship of time, internal control, and risk. This is the strategic thinking framework of senior management, and if internal auditors are going to support the goals and objectives of the organization, they will all need to learn to think with the strategic focus of senior management.

CHAPTER 3
THE ROLE OF CONTROL

Control is a term used to describe a process to mitigate risk. If risks are obstacles in achieving our goals and objectives, then controls are enablers. Controls prevent the consequences of risk events from affecting operations, or controls detect when the risks have affected the management process and alert management to the need for corrective action. A simple physical example is the controls in an aircraft. Some controls prevent the risk of error, such as the preflight checklist. Other controls detect the risk of error, such as navigation controls, and allow the pilot to correct the course. Controls are designed into systems to deny risk consequences the opportunity to affect operations (preventive control) and to provide feedback when certain risk consequences do affect operations (detective control).

The models below show the action of control (comparison to standard of *what should be*) in both preventive and detective modes. There are also other variations on these two basic structures, but in general, they accomplish control in these two ways.

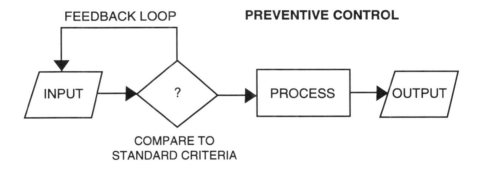

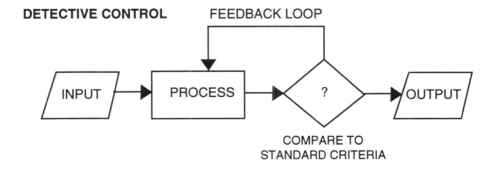

CONTROLS OVER RISKS SHOULD SUPPORT THE BUSINESS PROCESS

POSITIVE CONTROL +

CONTROL BOUNDARY

PROCESS 2

THE BUSINESS PROCESS

OUTSIDE
SUPPLIER

PROCESS 1

PROCESS 5

PROCESS 6

BUSINESS

GOALS

PROCESS 3

PROCESS 4

CONTROL BOUNDARY

NEUTRAL CONTROL

NEGATIVE CONTROL

Controls have efficiency ratings, depending upon how they affect the operation of the business process. Neutral controls have no effect. They keep the process from exceeding the boundaries defined by senior management, but the controls neither hinder nor help the process in relation to achieving goals. Negative controls act as "speed bumps" to the process. Negative controls create friction that slows the business process from reaching its objectives. "Red tape" is characteristic of negative controls. Positive controls tend to assist the business process in meeting its goals. Desirable controls are those that have a positive or neutral effect on the business process. Careful control design is important to maintain efficiency and effectiveness of the control system.

COSO

There are a number of important models of internal control; however, the dominant model in use today is the COSO model. The Com-

mittee of Sponsoring Organizations (COSO) was the first general model of internal control to be accepted by a wide professional audience.[1] COSO published *Internal Control - Integrated Framework* in 1992. At the same time, similar efforts were underway in Canada (the CICA Criteria on Control Committee - CoCo) and in the UK (the Cadbury Commission).

COSO is an important step in understanding internal control. One of the most important concepts in COSO is the principle of universal applicability: the internal control process

[1]The sponsors of COSO are the American Accounting Association (academia), the AICPA (public accountants), the Financial Executives Institute (treasurers/CFOs), The Institute of Internal Auditors, and the Institute of Management Accountants (corporate accountants). Because the AICPA have incorporated COSO into their standards, major accounting firms worldwide have adopted COSO. The IIA, another worldwide body, has also helped spread the influence of COSO beyond the borders of the U.S.

contains the same elements at the lowest level of the organization as it does in the highest level. Therefore, control and risk assessments that are carried out at lower levels have validity when aggregated ("rolled up") through lines of organization to the top. Thus control and risk assessments can be additive to a summary report of internal control and risk suitable for senior management and the board of directors' audit committee.

COSO is not perfect, but because COSO was first, and because it has been endorsed widely, COSO will be used as a general model to discuss internal control and risk. One other small flaw in COSO and the other control models is that they all look at control of operations from a financial bias instead of a general business perspective, largely because most of the research and effort came from the accounting profession.

The COSO report defines internal control as a "process, effected by an entity's board of directors, management and other personnel, which is designed to provide reasonable assurance regarding the achievement of objectives in one or more categories:

- Effectiveness and efficiency of **operations**.

- Reliability of **financial reporting**.
- **Compliance** with applicable laws and regulations."[2]

These three categories of control (Operations, Financial, Compliance) encompass all of the entity's activities. There was an addendum published May 1994 that clarified these internal control categories for management reporting on control activities should include safeguarding assets from loss or unauthorized use. This brought the COSO report into alignment with requirements under the U.S. Foreign Corrupt Practices Act section on the responsibilities for management reporting on internal control.

The COSO report describes internal control as having five components:

- Monitoring.
- Information and Communication.
- Control Activities.
- Risk Assessment.
- Control Environment.

These five components form the layers of internal control that cut across the three internal control objectives in a matrix:

	Operations	Financial Reporting	Compliance
Monitoring			
Information and Communication			
Control Activities			
Risk Assessment			
Control Environment			

[2]Committee of Sponsoring Organizations of the Treadway Commission, *Internal Control — Integrated Framework*; New York: COSO, 1992, p. 1.

Of the five components of control, two are additions to the traditional concepts of internal control, the elements of risk assessment and the control environment:

Risk assessment is recognized as a precondition of control selection. That is, you need to know and assess the risks before building the specific control activities. Some risk is also mitigated by the strength of the control environment.

"Control environment — The control environment sets the tone of an organization, influencing the control consciousness of its people. It is the foundation of all other components of internal control, providing discipline and structure. Control environment factors include integrity, ethical values and competence of the entity's people; management's philosophy and operating style; the way management assigns authority and responsibility, and organizes and develops its people; and the attention and direction provided by the board of directors."[3]

The basic COSO sequence is as follows:

Step One: Establish Objectives

According to the COSO approach, the first step in determining the controls required for a process is to establish the business objectives of the process. The purpose of internal control is to ensure that established objectives are achieved. In order to fulfill that purpose, the objectives need to be identified and agreed to by all participants in the organization. All risk assessment must begin with this first step.

In North America, some managers include Malcolm Baldrige criteria to supplement internal control objectives. Rank Xerox in the UK uses a number of models to establish their business objectives, including the Deming, Baldrige, and European Quality Award criteria. In Europe, where quality (ISO 9000) issues are more prevalent, there is a bias to include both internal control objectives and quality objectives in control and risk assessments:

> "...It is arguable that any ... assessment programme must include an assessment of both control *and quality* as quality management is inseparable from control management — both provide reasonable assurance of the achievement of business objectives..."[4]

Step Two: Assess Risk

The second step in the COSO sequence is to assess risk. Risk assessment is the identification, measurement, and prioritization of likely events (risks and opportunities) that may have a material consequence for the organization. The risks to be assessed are not *all* risks, but only those risks likely to create problems for the organization in trying to reach its objectives.

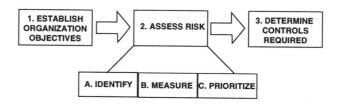

Step Three: Determine Controls Required

The process should determine the controls required to mitigate the risks identified. In con-

---

[3]Committee of Sponsoring Organizations of the Treadway Commission, *op. cit.*, p. 2.

[4]Institute of Internal Auditors - UK, *Control Self Assessment and Internal Audit* (Professional Briefing Note Seven), London: IIA - UK, 1995, p. 8.

trol design, the effort should be to design as few controls as possible, since each control consumes some amount of resources. Controls should be operating only for the risks with consequences that are material to reaching the goals and objectives. Excess controls are all negative ("speed bumps").

CoCo

The Canadian Institute of Chartered Accountants Criteria of Control Committee (CoCo) has been developing an internal control model that is similar to COSO, but with some significant differences.[5] Although using the same components of control, CoCo focuses on asking four important questions:

1. Do we have the right objectives?
2. Do we have the appropriate control activities?
3. Do we have the capability, the commitment, and the right environment in place?
4. Do we monitor, learn, and adapt?

CoCo builds on COSO foundations by identifying the same control components, but CoCo takes COSO a step further by looking at the *appropriateness* of the objectives and the control activities. Also, CoCo stresses capability and commitment as important parts of the control environment component. Coco stretches the monitoring component to include elements of the learning organization, thus allowing for a control environment that supports continuous improvement as well as protection from the negative consequences of business risk.

Like COSO, the CoCo model can be applied anywhere in the organization, at any level, which makes it possible to aggregate the responses into an entity-wide assessment of internal control and risk.

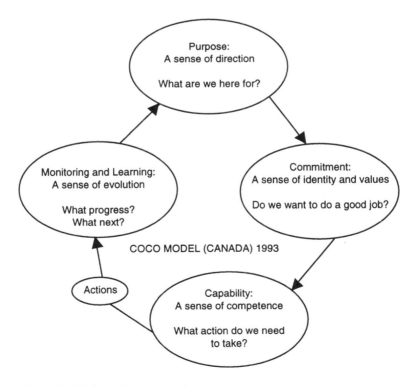

COCO MODEL (CANADA) 1993

---

[5]See Galloway, Duncan J., *Control Models in Perspective, Internal Auditor*, December 1994, pp.46-52.

The Criteria: The CoCo Guidance on Control[6]

PURPOSE

A1   Objectives should be established and communicated.

A2   The significant internal and external risks faced by an organization in the achievement of its objectives should be identified and assessed.

A3   Policies designed to support the achievement of an organization's objectives and the management of its risks should be established, communicated, and practised so that people understand what is expected of them and the scope of their freedom to act.

A4   Plans to guide efforts in achieving the organization's objectives should be established and communicated.

A5   Objectives and related plans should include measurable performance targets and indicators.

COMMITMENT

B1   Shared ethical values, including integrity, should be established, communicated and practised throughout the organization.

B2   Human resource policies and practices should be consistent with an organization's ethical values and with the achievement of its objectives.

B3   Authority, responsibility and accountability should be clearly defined and consistent with an organization's objectives so that decisions and actions are taken by the appropriate people.

B4   An atmosphere of mutual trust should be fostered to support the flow of information between people and their effective performance toward achieving the organization's objectives.

CAPABILITY

C1   People should have the necessary knowledge, skills and tools to support the achievement of the organization's objectives.

C2   Communication processes should support the organization's values and the achievement of its objectives.

C3   Sufficient and relevant information should be identified and communicated in a timely manner to enable people to perform their assigned responsibilities.

C4   The decisions and actions of different parts of the organization should be coordinated.

C5   Control activities should be designed as an integral part of the organization, taking into consideration its objectives, the risks to their achievement, and the interrelatedness of control elements.

MONITORING AND LEARNING

D1   External and internal environments should be monitored to obtain information that may signal a need to reevaluate the organization's objectives or control.

D2   Performance should be monitored against the targets and indicators identified in the organization's objectives and plans.

D3   The assumptions behind an organization's objectives and systems should be periodically challenged.

D4   Information needs and related information systems should be reassessed as objectives change or as reporting deficiencies are identified.

D5   Follow-up procedures should be established and performed to ensure appropriate change or action occurs.

D6   Management should periodically assess the effectiveness of control in its organization and communicate the results to those to whom it is accountable.

---

[6]Extracted from CICA *Guidance on Control*, an exhibit from Jackson, Peter, *Overview of CoCo*, Chicago, IL: IIA Control Assessment Conference Notes, 1995.

Cadbury and Other National Models

The Cadbury Commission in the UK has focused their effort on defining internal financial control; nevertheless, they have developed a control model that is very close to the general model used by COSO.[7] The Cadbury model includes safeguarding assets as part of the effective and efficient operations, unlike the original version of COSO. One other feature found in Cadbury that is not explicit in COSO is protecting records against concealment of theft or distortion of financial results as part of the financial reporting component. Cadbury also includes information systems throughout the control structure instead of separately treating the subject as it is done in the COSO model.

Monitoring and Corrective Action
Control Activities
Identification of Risks, Control Priorities, and Objectives
The Control Environment

Cadbury Commission (UK) 1994

The differences of the Cadbury model from COSO mean that control and risk assessments using Cadbury as the control framework would raise somewhat different questions. Also, the emphasis on financial internal control in Cadbury limits its usefulness as a general control framework. If using Cadbury, the practi-

tioner should consider using a general business control model (Malcolm Baldrige, for example) as a supplement to the financial control framework of Cadbury.

IIA Australia is leading the effort to develop its own version of a control framework. Their model is very much like CoCo. The South Africans are also reportedly developing a control model.

All models of internal control are helpful. Each one acts as a control checklist to ensure that all aspects of a business process are well defined, that controls can be examined for their efficiency, and that the control system as a whole can be judged on effectiveness in mitigating the identified risks so that business goals and objectives are achieved. In addition to the financially derived models, there is another group derived from the quality management movement.

Malcolm Baldrige Award Criteria and ISO 9000-Series Standards

The Malcolm Baldrige National Quality Award criteria are used by many organizations as their business control framework or as part of their total control framework. The NQA is sponsored by the U.S. government and administered by the American Society for Quality Control of Milwaukee, Wisconsin.

---

[7]Internal Control Working Group, *Internal Control and Financial Reporting* (Draft Response to the Cadbury Committee Report), London, UK: Institute of Chartered Accountants in England and Wales, October 1993.

International standards ISO 9000 series and the various national equivalents are occasionally used by organizations as part of their control framework. ISO standards ensure that the organization consistently produces products and services that meet customer specifications. ISO 9000 series (ISO 9001, 9002, 9003, 9004) define quality system standards, including documentation and monitoring systems. ISO 10011 defines guidelines for auditing quality systems designed and operated under ISO 9001-9003.[8]

REFERENCE	DESCRIPTION OF INTERNATIONAL STANDARD
ISO 9000	Quality Management and Quality Assurance Standards: Guidelines for using ISO 9001-9002-9003
ISO 9001	Quality Systems: Model for quality assurance in design, development, production, installation, and servicing
ISO 9002	Quality Systems: Model for quality assurance in production and installation
ISO 9003	Quality Systems: Model for quality assurance in final inspection and test
ISO 9004	Quality Management and Quality System Elements
ISO 10011	Guidelines for Auditing Quality Systems

---

[8]Chart adapted from De Meulder, Roland, *Meeting the Challenge of ISO, Internal Auditor*, April 1993, p.30.

1998 Malcolm Baldrige National Quality Award Categories		1000 Points
1.0	**LEADERSHIP**	**110**
	1.1 Leadership System 80	
	1.2 Company Responsibility and Citizenship 30	
2.0	**STRATEGIC PLANNING**	**80**
	2.1 Strategy Development Process 40	
	2.2 Company Strategy 40	
3.0	**CUSTOMER AND MARKET FOCUS**	**80**
	3.1 Customer and Market Knowledge 40	
	3.2 Customer Satisfaction and Relationship Enhancement 40	
4.0	**INFORMATION AND ANALYSIS**	**80**
	4.1 Selection and Use of Information and Data 25	
	4.2 Selection and Use of Comparative Information and Data 15	
	4.3 Analysis and Review of Company Performance 40	
5.0	**HUMAN RESOURCE FOCUS**	**100**
	5.1 Work Systems 40	
	5.2 Employee Education, Training, and Development 30	
	5.3 Employee Well-Being and Satisfaction 30	
6.0	**PROCESS MANAGEMENT**	**100**
	6.1 Management of Product and Service Processes 60	
	6.2 Management of Support Processes 20	
	6.3 Management of Supplier and Partnering Processes 20	
7.0	**BUSINESS RESULTS**	**450**
	7.1 Customer Satisfaction Results 125	
	7.2 Financial and Market Results 125	
	7.3 Human Resource Results 50	
	7.4 Supplier and Partner Results 25	
	7.5 Company-Specific Results 125	

CHAPTER 4
BUSINESS RISK ASSESSMENT

Business risk assessment refers to the assessment of risks and opportunities affecting the achievement of the organization's goals and objectives. Risk is assessed at three levels:

- **Strategic:** Used to guide the organization over a time period of five to 10 years. This assessment is usually performed by the senior management team.
- **Project/Program/Process:** Used to develop and manage the current period of organizational activity. The project/program/process manager is the person usually responsible for the initial assessment. He or she may also be responsible for monitoring project risk, or that may be shared with a project oversight committee.
- **Operational:** Used in everyday operations, largely a health and safety issue. This assessment is usually performed at the supervisory level or by individuals or work teams tasked with a particular assignment.

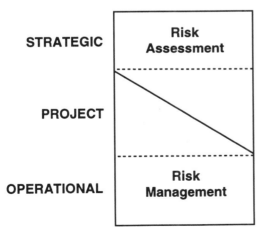

Strategic risk assessment is usually limited to assessment (the identification, measurement,

and prioritization of risks). Operational risk assessment usually focuses on risk management (standard workplace risks and hazards have already been identified; the task is to manage the risk to get the job done). Project risk assessment has a blend of both: risk assessment in the planning phase and risk management in the implementation phase.

Business risk assessment at all three levels is essential to identify the threats, opportunities, and alternatives for action to achieve the organization's goals and objectives.

Strategic Risk Assessment

The process of strategic risk assessment includes these six steps:

1. Gain an understanding of the organization's overall goals and objectives:
   - Examine the fundamental documents (mission statement, purpose statement, vision, or other fundamental document) for goals and objectives. There are typically three to seven of these.
   - Classify each of the identified goals and objectives into short, medium, and long-term issues. Most mission statements will have some of each of these.

2. Choose the strategic risks that are likely to be of greatest importance to the organization:
   - Operational Risk: The risk that the entity will not meet its operational goals and objectives.
   - Fiscal Risk: The risk that deficiencies in expenditure control or revenues will adversely affect agreed-upon outcomes or objectives.

- Reputation Risk: The risk that some action or inaction by the entity will impair the organization's ability to reach its goals and objectives.
- Other strategic risks, such as Policy Risk, Regulatory Risk, etc.

3. Define the various environments that are important to the organization, such as:
   - Political/Government.
   - Technology.
   - Legal and Regulatory.
   - Competitors.
   - Customers, Constituents, and Stakeholders.
   - Physical.

- Markets.
- Suppliers.
- Economic/Financial.

Each of these "environments" represents a bundle of uncertainties generally associated with that area.

4. Create a series of matrices, with Strategic Risk Areas put at the top axis, and Environments along the side axis. The matrices should be in a "set" of three; that is, for each issue identified in step 1 (Goals and Objectives), there should be a matrix to record the risks focusing on short term, medium-term and long-term issues.

GOAL: _____   Time Horizon: _____

Environments	Strategic Risk	Operations Risk	Fiscal Risk	Reputation Risk
Physical				
Economic/Financial				
Customers				
Competitors				
Legal/Regulatory				
Technology				
Suppliers				

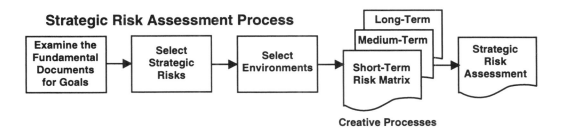

Strategic Risk Assessment Process

Examine the Fundamental Documents for Goals → Select Strategic Risks → Select Environments → [Long-Term / Medium-Term / Short-Term Risk Matrix] → Strategic Risk Assessment

Creative Processes

5. Using various creative processes such as brainstorming, imagine scenarios of possible threats and opportunities for each of the cells on the matrix. It is important to think "outside the box" as much as possible — some organizations use an outside consultant to help break through any preconceptions and bias. Use tools such as multi-voting to pare the list of threats and opportunities to the most significant (a combination of most likely and those with the largest impact). Because not every environment affects every strategic risk area, not every cell will have data.

6. Combine the risk assessments for various goals and objectives for each of the three time horizons to get a composite strategic risk assessment. Based on the assessment of likely scenarios, managers can then plan to deal with those risks.

Project Risk Assessment

Project risk assessment uses a different method to identify risk and opportunity. Project risk identification uses one or more of the following methods:

- Exposure Analysis: Risk from the perspective of the assets involved.
- Environmental Analysis: Risk from the perspective of the changes in environments. This method is the same as that used in strategic risk assessment.

- Threat Scenarios: Risk explored from various narrative scenarios of what might happen under a number of conditions. This is helpful for exploring catastrophic events and frauds.

Risk is difficult to observe or measure directly, so "risk factors" are used that are either observable or measurable characteristics of conditions at risk. A standard set of risk factors and criteria should be established to measure and rank projects according to their perceived risk.

Each project, program, or process to be formally assessed for risk should be scored by the project initiator with the established risk factors based on an understanding of the project, program, or process and the perception of risk as described. The scores should be in the range of 1 (Lowest Risk) to 5 (Highest Risk). Projects, programs, or processes may be scored by a number of individuals and averaged, or this process can be used to score multiple projects for purposes of relative risk ranking (such evaluating various operational alternatives, including the risk of not doing anything). The process depends on a thorough understanding of the details of the project, program, or process as well as a thorough understanding of the organization's business process and political context. If the project manager is not familiar with the prerequisite knowledge, others should participate in the risk assessment.

Procedures:

A. Identify Risk
1. Use one or more methods to identify risk (exposure analysis, environmental analysis, or threat scenarios).

B. Measure Risk/Develop Alternatives
2. Read each factor and sub-criteria to familiarize yourself with the aim of each.
3. Consider the project, program, or process using each of the factors/criteria.
4. Score each factor for the project, etc. on a scale of 1 to 5 (Lowest to Highest) based on your subjective assessment of the strength/weakness or presence/absence of the criteria.
5. Sum the scores for each factor and divide by the number of factors to get the average score.

6. High-risk scores are those with an average of 4.25 or more. Low risk scores are those with an average score of less than 2.25. These are starting figures that can be adjusted for experience.
7. Analyze the high-risk areas and develop alternatives (controls or other risk management techniques) to deal with each of the high risk components.
8. Price out the alternatives and compare risks and costs.

C. Control Design
9. Choose the most cost-effective controls within reasonable prudence and organizational tolerance for accepting risk.

D. Risk Management
10. Monitor risks and hazards, making adjustments to the project plan as necessary to meet changing conditions.

Project Risk Assessment/Risk Management

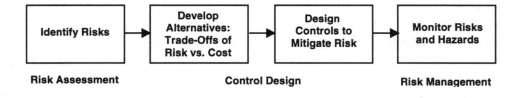

Operational Risk Management

Operational risk is the day-to-day mitigation of safety and health risks of employees performing their jobs. Operational risk also covers visitors and temporary workers in the workplace and risks to the general public due to operations. The focus of operational risk is on risk management. Risk assessment is usually done by a specialist involved in workplace risks:

- Health risks, including exposure to toxins, radiation, and infectious organisms.
- Safety risks, including exposure to equipment, machinery, and work processes.
- Environmental/physical risks, including exposure to climate and terrain.

CHAPTER 5
RISK IDENTIFICATION

The key to risk assessment is the identification of threats and opportunities. Risk cannot be measured, prioritized, or managed until it has been identified. Risk identification involves speculating about the relevant threats (and possibly opportunities) that could affect an organization and its ability to achieve its business goals. The three main approaches to risk identification are:

Exposure Analysis: The identification of risks that could affect assets.

Environmental Analysis: The identification of risks that could affect operations.

Threat Scenarios: Specialized risk identification for frauds and/or disasters.

The choice of which one of these approaches is most appropriate depends upon the nature of the organization. In any case, risk identification is often done using all three approaches (one primary method is chosen, and the other two methods are used to ensure a complete picture is available for planning).

The Exposure Approach

Managers put assets at risk to achieve objectives. One of the three major approaches to identifying risk is the exposure approach or exposure analysis. In the exposure approach, the focus is on the assets at risk in the process:

- **Physical assets** such as plant and equipment.
- **Financial assets** such as cash and investments.
- **Human assets** including the knowledge and experience of the staff.
- **Intangible assets** such as information, reputation, brand recognition.

The exposure approach takes into consideration the Size, Type, Portability, and Location (STPL) of the assets. Threats and risks are explored which could materially affect the assets. The exposure approach works best on those processes that depend heavily on their assets for goal achievement. Examples of asset-intensive organizations/units:

- Manufacturing processes.
- Construction (and salvage) operations.
- Cashiering operations.
- Motor vehicle fleet operations.
- Inventory processes.
- Research and development activities.
- Software systems development activities.

How it works:

1. The process includes some key assets. Those assets are identified by size, type, portability, and location (STPL).

   Example: An audit has been assigned to review remodeling expenses for expanded office space. The major assets involved are Building Materials and Current Office Space. Some of the building materials are small and valuable (fixtures), some are small and immaterial (nails, etc.), and some are large and valuable (wood paneling). All materials are stored within the office building. The Office Space is an asset that is used to achieve the current objectives. The Current Office Space is exposed to loss through excessive noise and disruption during remodeling.

2. Speculation is generated about how these assets are exposed to loss of value or impairment/loss of utility to accomplish the objectives.

	Risks of Loss	Risks of Impairment
Small, portable, immaterial	N.M.*	N.M.*
Small, portable, valuable	Theft, fire, handling damage	Handling damage
Large, valuable	Fire, handling damage	Handling damage
Current Office Space	Fire, extended power outage	Noise, excessive dust, power fluctuations

* = Not Meaningful

Example: Use a matrix of assets along one axis and the two negative consequences, Loss and Impairment, along another axis to ensure that both risks to all major assets are explored. What we are trying to generate is a list of risks that could cause these consequences to these assets.

The risks that were identified in the example through the exposure approach (in order of frequency) were:

1. Handling damage   4. Theft

2. Fire   5. Noise

3. Power outages   6. Excessive dust

Even though there are some assets classified as small and portable, certain assets in this group were found to be immaterial, or at least not worth special risk analysis.

Note that there are more components to remodeling than are included in this list of assets. In every audit there will be assets to be considered to some extent. Also, in nearly every audit there will be other sources of risk as well. That is why it is recommended to use at least two of the three (if not all three) of the

major risk identification approaches to ensure that all significant risk has been considered. The other two approaches, the Environmental Approach and Threat Scenarios, will round out the risk identification process.

The Environmental Approach

The organization exists in an external environment made up of many other environments, such as:

- **Physical** environment: Site, location, weather, terrain, access.
- **Economic** environment: Finances, interest rates, general economy.
- **Government regulation**: Laws, policies, and regulations — real or impending.
- **Competition**: Direct competitors, substitutions, indirect competitors.
- **Constituents/Customers**.
- **Suppliers (including Unions)**.
- **Technology**.

The environmental approach seeks to consider risk arising from various states of the environment, both the current state and the future states. Threats and risks are explored which could materially affect the accomplishment of objectives. The environmental approach works best in service-oriented processes and those that are highly regulated or competitive, although nearly every organization is affected by environmental risk to some extent.

Examples of organizations/units where the environmental approach works well include:

- Sales, marketing and distribution functions.
- Bank operations.
- Customer-facing/customer service activities.
- Government and public utility operations.
- Internal service functions (legal, accounting, etc.).

How it works:

1. The process is affected by a number of external environmental issues. These issues are identified from the list of environments.

   Example: An audit of bank 24-hour telephone customer services has been assigned.

Surveying the environments, several are identified as having some impact on customer service:

- Customer perceptions and customer attitudes.
- Competitors and competitor advertising.
- Physical environment of customer interaction (via telephone).

2. Speculation is generated about what the state of these environments are now and how they might change in the near future (both "what is" and "what could happen") in terms of consequences to our unit's objectives of customer service.

   Example: Use a matrix of environments along one axis and the two states of the environment, Now and Future, to explore the consequences and risks. What we are trying to generate is a list of risks that could cause these consequences to meeting our customer service objectives.

	Current Environment "What Is"	Future Environment "What Could Happen"
Customers	Customers leave	Unable to attract new customers
Competitors	Match hours and levels of service	Try to attract our customers
Physical	Vulnerable to telephone rate changes	Internet access becomes competitive standard for physical access to services

The risks and threats in our simple example would lead us to an audit program that ensured the organization was keeping current with market intelligence as to customer perceptions and customer needs as well as competitive responses. The possible changes to the physical access to customer service, either its cost or its methodology, should be addressed in the unit's business plan.

Environmental analysis is much more subjective than the Exposure Approach. The speculation is multidimensional; therefore, this type of speculation is best done in collaboration with others, including management. Also note that our example was simplified to illustrate the method of the approach. Many organizations have significant regulatory concerns, supplier relations, and even international environmental/competitive issues.

In planning an individual audit, it is usually most efficient to start with either the asset Exposure Approach or the external Environmental Approach and then switch around and do it the other way to round out the identification of significant risk.

The Threat Scenario Approach

The third major approach to risk identification is the Threat Scenario Approach. This is most useful when dealing with fraud or security issues. Many risk assessments start with one of the other two methods (Exposure Analysis, Environmental Analysis, or both) and then perform a special scenario building process to deal with fraud and security.

Threat scenarios can be used for basic risk assessment in the audit as well. The reason that scenarios are not used as frequently as the other two approaches is the time and skills required to do the job properly. Threat scenarios need someone with a lot of expertise, either someone from the process or an experienced auditor (preferably both).

Threat scenarios are bound by time periods. That is, each scenario has to reflect a certain time period, since the consequences of realized threats change over time. Threat scenarios may be for specific times, such as for computer outage where time is measured in hours. Threat scenarios also may be made for time periods such as short-term, mid-term, and long-term scenarios.

Short-term threats (the most common scenario) can be classified as:

- Errors
- Delays
- Omissions
- Fraud

How it works:

Scenarios are narrative descriptions of the process and the assets at risk, as well as the possible things that could go wrong (consequences). Often these narratives include the mitigating control system description as well.

1. The process is carefully documented, either in narrative form or "portfolio" form. Portfolio form is easier to manipulate by a computer, since only minimum data are collected. The Lawrence Livermore Risk Analysis Model (LRAM), created by Charles Cresson Wood, uses a portfolio approach which captures:

- Asset description.
  Example: Mainframe computer.

- Specific threat.
  Example: Water damage.

- Consequences of that threat on that asset.
  Example: Unavailability, replacement/ repair costs, and cost of alternative/ backup facilities.

- How the threat is typically realized. *Example:* Roof leaks onto equipment below. Flooding could also be a typical water damage threat, depending on location.

2. If the major purpose of the scenario is the threat of fraud, the scenario's "how realized" must cover the three elements of fraud:

   - Theft: How the asset could be stolen.
   - Concealment: How the theft could be concealed or go undetected.
   - Conversion: How the theft could be converted to personal use.

   NOTE: If threat scenarios are used to audit and evaluate fraud and security issues, the scenarios become a blueprint for crime. This documentation should be properly secured when not in use.

3. Once the risks are identified, the auditor looks for controls that are missing and designs tests for the rest to ensure that they are actually working as intended.

Exercise: Three-Way Risk Identification

The purpose of this exercise is to gain practice in identifying risk using the three methods: Exposure Analysis, Environmental Analysis, and Threat Scenarios.

Background

The New Western Bank headquarters Branch Banking Unit was responsible for overseeing the operations of 34 branch banking locations throughout the western part of the country. The branches provided consumer and small business banking services in their local territories, including taking deposits, making loans, and providing miscellaneous fee services.

Branch banking was a highly competitive business in this area, and major banks were always looking for successful regionals like New Western as possible acquisition candidates. New Western has been growing at 12% per year compounded over the past five years. An average of six new branches had been added each year over that time. Operations are highly customer-focused. Each branch manager establishes a personal banking relationship with major customers, both depositors and borrowers.

New products are developed by headquarters and "rolled out" to the branches for marketing at an average of one every two months.

Each year, the New Western selects approximately two-thirds of all branches for audit. The strategy was to audit each branch at least three times every two years. The main purpose of the audit was to ensure that the branch complies with all government regulations and company policies. To achieve this purpose, the auditors use a standard audit procedure manual to perform audits of the branch operations. In addition to compliance, there is a considerable risk of fraud. There have been complaints by auditors and branch managers that the audit manual is outdated and focuses effort on the wrong things.

Required

Your team has been asked to come up with a risk-based branch audit manual, so that the audits can be more efficient and effective. As part of this effort, your group must identify the major sources of risk for the standard branch audit in the following format:

Risk Profile: Branch Banking

Exposure Analysis:

    Risk Source   **Why?**

Environmental Analysis:

    Risk Source   **Why?**

Threat Scenarios:

    Risk Source   **Why?**

Identifying Inherent Risk: Generating Ideas

In the third part of Risk Identification, the auditor is supposed to "identify the inherent business risks." Two things are required:

- A thorough understanding of the business processes of the organization or audible unit.
- A means to generate a reasonable list of possible risks.

Generating ideas about risks is a creative process of discovery. It requires some imagination of "what could go wrong" in the process as well as good research skills. The common methods of identifying possible risks are:

- Analogies to similar operations.
  Example: Review of software applications in one unit can often be helpful in identifying generic sources of risk in software applications in other units.

- Prior history of the operation or audible unit.
  Example: Prior working papers or audit reports or other documentation reveal certain risks inherent in that operation.

- Industry surveys about critical issues.
  Example: Common threats to operations such as government regulation of the industry.

- Trade or business magazine articles about other organizations' performing that process.
  Example: Mishandling volatile derivatives in the investment portfolio of one county should alert all other entities that investment portfolio guidelines and operations need to be reviewed.

- Common sense or experience.
  Example: The risk of theft of cash in a cash handling operation.

The Texas Instruments Brainstorming Approach

Texas Instruments (TI), and a number of other internal audit groups, use a highly efficient and effective approach to generating the possible risks about an organization or audible unit. Many audit managers give a lot of information and background when they assign audit projects. Some auditors use electronic mail or other means to query other auditors about their knowledge of the audit subject, the risks, the controls, or the organization. Texas Instruments enhances the audit assignment process by using a formal/informal brainstorming session. When an audit is assigned at TI, the auditor sets up a quick meeting with everyone in the office at that time for a focused 30-minute brainstorming session where they try to identify (in 10 minutes each):

- Risks associated with the process.
- Expected controls in the process.
- Probable weaknesses in control.

The auditors share their experience and knowledge, and the assignment becomes more focused and efficient as a result of this teamwork. The time limit ensures that the team does not waste resources during the exercise, nor is it burdensome for anyone.

TI and other workgroups also try to include management of the audible unit in their session whenever possible to ensure that some critical part of the business process is not overlooked or played down. This is also a good example of using collaboration in risk assessment to make the audit process more efficient and effective.

NOTE: Internal auditors do not normally invite management representatives into brainstorming sessions that involve a surprise audit like cash counts. Such audits can be planned with management's participation; however, this will usually involve someone from central staff rather than the custodian of the cash.

A Framework for Risk Identification

A framework for risk identification is shown on the following page. The diagram provides a stimulator to examine all aspects of risk in the entity:

- Identifying the major assets (exposure approach).
- Identifying the major environmental influences (environmental approach).
- Identifying the major processes and objectives (threat scenarios).

RISK ASSESSMENT APPROACH

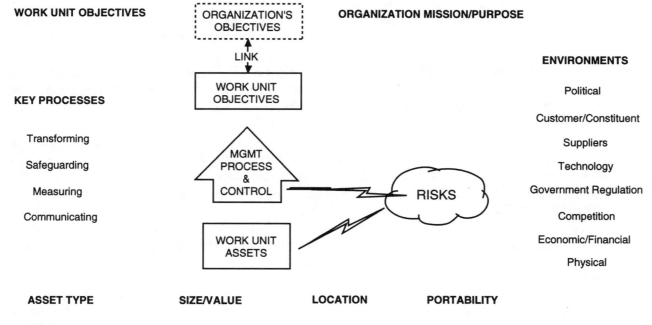

WORK UNIT OBJECTIVES

ORGANIZATION'S OBJECTIVES

ORGANIZATION MISSION/PURPOSE

LINK

WORK UNIT OBJECTIVES

ENVIRONMENTS

Political

KEY PROCESSES

Customer/Constituent

Transforming

Suppliers

MGMT PROCESS & CONTROL

Safeguarding

Technology

Measuring

RISKS

Government Regulation

Communicating

Competition

Economic/Financial

WORK UNIT ASSETS

Physical

ASSET TYPE	SIZE/VALUE	LOCATION	PORTABILITY

Physical:

Financial:

Human:

Information/Intangible:

Exercise: Operational Risk Identification

> The purpose of this exercise is to gain experience in identifying the source of risks in an operational context.

Background

The Global Insurance Company was in a very competitive market. Because the financial markets were relatively stable, margins on underwriting income were vitally important. The company was locked in a three-way duel with First Assurance and Second Mutual Insurance for underwriting business. The company also was looking at every expense as an opportunity to fatten the margins.

Among the expenses the company reviewed was the garbage and waste disposal fees. The company rented a mid-size trash hopper from the city collection service. Analyzing the volume of trash, the company determined that it was:

- 83% white paper   (1,250 lbs. per week)
- 9% colored paper
- 8% other (plastics, metals, garbage).

The company generated a lot of paper in the course of business. Senior management decided to change this expense into a new revenue stream for the company. Starting the first of next month, the company would auction its paper to recyclers. The auction would be for a 12-month contract to collect and dispose of the company's waste white paper. The new process would require the company's personnel to separate recyclable white paper from the other trash.

Due to privacy laws, the company was responsible to see that no personal information was disclosed in the disposal process. The contract would require the vendor to shred all paper before it was resold to the pulp and paper mill. The vendor would also be required to furnish receptacles to separate the trash. Projected savings from reducing the trash collection charges from the city were $290 per month. Recycled paper was selling at $40 per ton.

Required

Management has asked your advice about the risks in establishing a recycling program. In your team, identify the risks in the above recycling scheme. Use this format:

Risk Profile: Global Insurance Co. Recycling Plan

Environmental Analysis:

    Risk Source

                    Why?

Exposure Analysis:

    Risk Source

                    Why?

Threat Scenarios:

    Risk Source

                    Why?

HINTS: This is an operational issue, and figures are readily available for a cost/benefit analysis. Also, ask yourself "What could go wrong?" and apply that knowledge to some asset or activity.

CHAPTER 6
RISK MEASUREMENT

Once the risks and consequences are identified, the next step is to measure them. Measuring risk is difficult because of its intangible nature. Mathematicians (and some accountants) are fond of using probability estimates for risk measurement. Managers (and most internal auditors) prefer to think of risk in qualitative rather than quantitative terms. For many managers, defining risk on a three-point scale (Low, Medium, High) is sufficient for their needs.

Measuring risk is not a precise science, nor need it be. Risk assessment aids in planning in that it helps identify parts of the plan that may need more attention than others because they are more important or less protected by controls. The risk assessment process gets the manager to the important parts of the decision process, but the manager makes adjustments and decisions based on the actual conditions encountered.

Risks are events with some probability of occurring. Consequences are the result of risks acting on our business processes and our goals and objectives. Both risks and their consequences are measurable over three dimensions:

1. Risk occurrence is a *probability* of the likelihood that the risk will create a consequence that could materially affect our ability to achieve our business goals.

   Example: A bank has a vault of registered securities with a fixed interest rate held as collateral against a loan. **The bank is at risk** if interest rates rise above a certain amount (the collateral no longer covers the value of the loan). Given reasonable record keeping, **the bank is not at risk** if the securities are physically damaged, even though that is a real risk with a reasonable probability of occurrence. The reason is that the risk of damage does not affect the bank's business process in a material way (the securities are registered, so they can be replaced if lost or damaged) **in spite of the likelihood of occurrence.**

2. The *severity of consequences* is another dimension of risk measurement. Severity of consequence is often dependent on the operation of internal controls. Some controls reduce the consequences to immaterial events. Consequences must have a material affect on the ability to achieve objectives. Risks with immaterial consequences, or with consequences that do not affect our ability to achieve our goals, are eliminated from consideration. Those internal controls that reduce consequences to immateriality are tested in the audit program.

   Example: Using the same bank example as above, the risk of loss or damage given adequate record keeping (the control) is not worth considering since the cost of replacement (the consequence) is not material. We would not design an audit program that covered all custodial controls against risk of physical damage or loss; however, we would verify that we have good record-keeping controls through an inventory test of the securities in the vault.

3. The *timing* of a risk and the *duration* of its consequence are the third dimension of risk measurement. Risks may have consequences that vary in severity depending on when in the business process they occur and how long the effect of the consequence lasts.

Example: Timing becomes an issue in computer operations. The risk of interruption of the bank's computer processing is greater during certain parts of the day (power grid load), certain times of the year (severe weather), and even certain processing sequences (highly complex operations requiring a lot of operator response). Probabilities of interruption from a number of causes rise and fall depending on these other factors.

Likewise, the duration of a consequence can affect the magnitude of the risk. Bank computer processing is usually driven by cycles. Disruption of these cycles for an hour is one level of risk; disruption for a day is another (higher) level of risk; and disruption for a week is likely to put the bank out of business.

Methods for Measuring Risk

There are several approaches to measuring the risks and consequences:

- **Direct probability estimates and expected loss functions:** The application of probabilities to asset values to determine exposure for loss.
- **Risk factors:** The use of observable factors to substitute for measuring a specific risk or class of risks.
- **Weighted matrices:** The use of threats x components matrices to evaluate consequences and controls.

Direct Probability Estimates

1. One approach assigns probability values to inherent risks, control risks, and audit risks. This is common in investment portfolio management and public accounting. This formula looks like:

$$Total\ Risk = IR \times CR \times AR$$

Inherent Risk (***IR***) takes on arbitrary values, according to guidelines set up by the public accounting bodies (Canadian Institute of Chartered Accountants recommend values of 0.40, 0.50, 0.60 for low, medium and high, and U.S. firms generally use values between 0.50, 0.75, and 1.00 respectively). Often Control Risk (***CR***) and Audit Risk (***AR***) are also arbitrarily assigned values to represent low, medium, and high levels of risk.

This equation is usually solved for the Audit Risk (Detection Risk) given an acceptable confidence level (90% confidence in the audit result = 0.10 Total Risk):

$$AR = \frac{Total\ Risk}{(IR \times CR)}$$

The weakness in this approach is that the various arbitrary values are tied to subjective estimates of what is "low," "medium," and "high" instead of the other way around: deriving the level or risk based on some estimate of probability.

Example: The auditor of the bank's cashiering operations assesses the inherent risk as high (risk of theft of cash), control risk as medium, and wants to have a 90% confidence in the audit work (Total Risk = 0.10):

$$AR = \frac{0.10}{1.00 \times 0.50} = 0.20\ (a\ relatively\ low\ detection\ risk)$$

As IR decreases (from certainty, 1.00, to values less than 1.00), less testing is required (more detection risk is taken).

A second weakness in using direct probability estimation is that senior management does not view risk in this manner. Most senior managers feel uncomfortable with probability statements, according to behavioral research. Managers prefer qualitative expressions about risk.

2. A second method of direct estimation is a consequence-driven estimate using an estimated annual loss function, also known as the **Annualized Loss Expectancy (ALE)**. This approach is relatively common among information systems auditors. The simplified formula is shown as:

$$Expected\ Loss = \sum_{i=1}^{N} P_i \times D_i \times V_i$$

The expected losses for threats in the system is the sum of the products of probability P times the duration D times the value of the assets V for all threats i (see chart below).

This sort of analysis is used by risk management for insurance purposes, as well as some internal auditors.

An enhancement on this approach takes into account the probability of control failure as well. The Annualized Loss Expectancy (ALE) for each scenario i by quantitatively expressing a probability of the threat occurring P^T, the probability of control failure P^F, and the maximum dollar loss of the consequence Q:

$$Total\ ALE = \sum_{i=1}^{N} (P^T_i \times P^F_i \times Q_i)$$

Example: The computer center contains a Central Computer Mainframe (CPU), Disk Storage devices (DASD), Tape Drives, Printers, and a Console. One scenario is electrical fire. The controls over such a risk include a fire suppressant system, handheld extinguishers, equipment tarps, fire alarms, 24-hour observation, and supplier agreements for 8-hour delivery of replacement parts for everything except the CPU (24-hour replacement guarantee).

Asset: Computer Center

Threats i	Probability P of Threat	Duration D (Days)	Value V of Asset	Expected Loss
Fire	.001	5	4,000,000	20,000
Flood	.005	3	4,000,000	60,000
Earthquake	.0001	10	4,000,000	4,000
Power Failure	.01	.1	4,000,000	4,000
TOTAL				88,000

The risks could be measured by a table such as the following:

Asset	Maximum Dollar Loss: Value at Risk Q	Probability of Threat Occurring P^T	Probability of Control Failure P^F	Annualized Loss Expectancy ALE
CPU	1,200,000	0.004	0.20	960
DASD	500,000	0.009	0.20	900
Tape Drives	300,000	0.006	0.20	360
Printers	150,000	0.012	0.20	360
Console	40,000	0.010	0.20	80
TOTAL	2,190,000			2,660

There should be a number of scenarios, each with its own table, to effectively evaluate the total annual expected losses from various risk sources. The cost of improving control reliability can be measured using a table such as this to give input to the decision on increased controls. Also, comparisons (e.g., DASD vs. CPU) can be made for deciding the relative extent of control testing to be done. In our example, the auditor might have planned to do more testing of the controls over the CPU than other components because of its dollar value; however, the highest loss potential is in the DASD.

Risk Factors

Risk measurement usually involves both subjective judgment and reference to objective or historical data. Often, the measurement of risk is accomplished by measuring a number of factors related to risk, such as:

- Complexity.
- Dollars at Risk.
- Liquidity of the Assets.
- Competence of Management.
- Strength of Internal Control.
- Time Since Last Audit.

Risk factors are ways of combining our thinking about risks, consequences, and controls all at once into observable events or conceptual attributes to allow risk to be more easily measured. Using risk factors for measuring risk is useful when the auditable units share a lot in common, as with branch banks, plants, divisions, or other location-based audits. Risk factors are also used in developing risk models for the annual audit plan. Generally, the more of a risk factor that is present, the higher the risk and/or consequence.

There are three types of risk factors commonly in use:

1. Subjective Risk Factors.
2. Objective or Historical Risk Factors.
3. Calculated Risk Factors.

Subjective Risk Factors:

Due to the rapid changes in the complexity of both technology and organizations over the past two decades, historical data has become less significant. Risk measurement and the identification of consequences require a combination of experience, skills, imagination, and creativity. This emphasis on subjective measurements is borne out in practice: many auditable units change so much between audits that prior audit history is of little use. Sound subjective judgment by an experienced practitioner is just as valid as any other method.

Example: Subjective Risk Factors

- Integrity of Management.
- Extent of Rapid Changes in Processes.

Objective or Historical Risk Factors:

For stable operations, measuring the trends in historical risk factors can be useful. In all cases, current objective data is very helpful in measuring risk.

Example: Objective and Historical Risk Factors

- Dollars at Risk (Objective).
- Employee Turnover Rates (Historical).

Calculated Risk Factors:

A subset of Objective risk factor data is the class of factors that are calculated from historical or objective data. These are often the weakest of all factors to use because they are derivative factors of risk further "upstream."

Example: Calculated Risk Factors

- Distance from Main Office.
- Time Since Last Audit.

Measuring Risk and Removing Bias from Subjective Risk Factors

Using risk factors means reliance on a number of subjective judgments about risk. Objective, Historical, and Calculated risk factors can be easily measured for use in a quantitative risk model.

Subjective risk factors are not as easily measured. In order to minimize the bias that comes with subjective risk assessment, several methods are recommended:

1. Statistical Measurements

   By using observable facts and data to correlate subjective estimates, statistical processes can be used to measure the subjective risk factor.

   Example: The Strength of Internal Control (a subjective risk factor) could be based on the number and severity of adverse audit findings. Regression or other factor analysis techniques are used to establish the strength of the correlation.

2. Pattern or Profile Measurements

   An attempt to classify subjective risk factors according to the aggregate risk pattern or "profile" that the unit has in relation to known risk standards. Thus a project's subjective risk factors might be measured by comparing the overall pattern of judgments against projects with similar features and similar judgments.

   Example: A pattern of controls and operating conditions in savings and loan lending in the past have shown that there are significant risks of fraud. The auditor compares the current lending controls and conditions of the bank with those known to harbor fraudulent transactions, and the auditor makes a judgment as to the risk of fraud based on that comparison.

3. Intuition

Studies have shown that experienced managers/analysts/auditors/technicians can use intuition to arrive at reasonable estimates of risk that cannot be measured accurately using only the five senses. This type of measurement must be done on site where the full range of influence can be perceived.

Example: The auditor visited the auditable unit's location and discussed the business issues and controls with managers and workers. Based on her experience, she "felt" that certain areas had more risk than others and wrote her audit program accordingly.

4. Group Processes

The Delphi Technique and other group decision tools are useful in pooling the experience and intuition of a larger group of experts. A consensus is built around an assessment based on expertise from several people. These consensus techniques help to minimize measurement bias by canceling out personal bias.

Example: Delphi is a nominal group process that uses experts who independently rate and rank a list of topics. Feedback is given on their rating and the group's rating. After several iterations, the advice tends to converge on a consensus.

Using and Weighing Risk Factors

Risk factors are identified or chosen to represent risks and consequences that have been identified. How to use them in an audit is a five-step process:

1. Choose a number of factors to represent important aspects of the auditable unit's risks. These factors should be **determinant**, that is, the measurements on these factors should vary from conditions of low risk to high risk. Limit risk factors to no more than 10. Using five, plus or minus two, should be your goal. The more factors, the more likely you are duplicating the influence of a particular risk, and the less influence any particular factor has on determining ultimate risk.

Example: The unit may have extraordinary pressures to meet goals. This pressure can cause some managers to cut corners or fabricate production statistics in an effort to meet unreasonably high objectives. Therefore, a reasonable risk factor that can be used to judge portions of the auditable unit's operations is how much pressure is being applied to which parts of the process: the more pressure, the higher the risk.

2. Choose a scale, such as "1-to-5," to represent the strength of the factors in the auditable unit (low-to-high). A five-point scale is recommended, although a three-point scale (low-medium-high, or weak-average-strong) or even a nine-point scale can be used. Some scales will be linear, and some will be not, depending on the nature of the factor and which part of the business process is being reviewed:

Example: If one Risk Factor is "Dollars at Risk" (an Objective, or easily measured factor), then the following examples demonstrate the variety of the scales and shapes of curves for different parts of the business cycle:

3. Evaluate each of the components of the auditable unit and assign a score based on your scale from step #2. Components of the auditable unit can be any or all of these in any mixture:

- Functions.
- Subprocesses.
- Software.

- Hardware, machines or other assets.
- People or positions.
- Procedures and policies.

Example: In the bank's Loan Application Unit, there are the following components:

- The mail clerk position.
- The loan officer position.
- Loan application and approval procedures manual.
- The loan committee.
- The loan screening software.

Each of these components was scored on each of five risk factors. The factors were:

- Pressure to meet objectives.
- Freedom to act.
- Decision support tools used by the position.
- Prior internal control weaknesses.
- Amount of supervisory review.

4. Develop weights for each of the risk factors chosen based on the impact (probability and consequences) that each factor has on the unit. It is good practice to normalize the weights; that is, to make sure that the sum of all weights adds up to 1.00 or 100%. A risk factor should have at least a 10% influence (0.10 weight) on the auditable unit if it is to be used. In a five-factor model, the risk factors typically range in weights from 0.10 minimum to 0.30 maximum (sometimes as much as 0.40, but rarely as much as 0.50).

Example: For our five risk factors in the example above in step #3, we could develop risk factor weights in either of two ways:

a. **Direct Assignment:** Using judgment to determine the weight a particular factor should have in relation to other factors. Direct assignment can be done by the auditor or by a group using a con-

sensus tool such as the Delphi Technique.

b. **Analytic Hierarchy Process:** Using a method of pair-wise comparisons (each factor is paired with every other factor) and expressing the strength of preference of one member of the pair over the other member. A series of pair-wise comparisons of all possible pairs results in a "chain of preference" that can be used to derive weights. This usually takes a computer to do, so Direct Assignment is the most popular and quicker method.

5. Multiply the factor score F given each component of the audit in step #3 times the weight W of each factor i in step #4 to get the score for each components. Sum the scores for each component (all factors times all weights). The components with the higher score are the ones with the most risk.

Example: The weighted risk score for a particular factor is:

$$Risk_i = W_i \times F_i$$

The sum of all five weighted risk scores equates to relative risk for that component.

$$Total\ Risk = \sum_{i=1}^{N} (W_i \times F_i)$$

The auditor then designs tests to deal with the relative risk distribution.

Large Physical Assets (Building, etc.):
Accounting/Treasury Functions:

SCALE   <$100,000   = 1
         $100,000 - $1 Million   = 2
         $1 M - $10 Million   = 3
         $10 M - $100 Million   = 4
         >$100 Million   = 5

Logarithmic Scale (Risk is Low except at Very High Values)

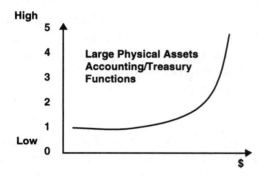

Small Physical Assets & Cash:
Revenue Functions:

SCALE   <$5,000   = 1
         $5,000 - $25,000   = 2
         $25,000 - $50,000   = 3
         $50,000 - $100,000 = 4
         >$100,000   = 5

Exponential Scale (Risk Climbs Quickly even at Low Values)

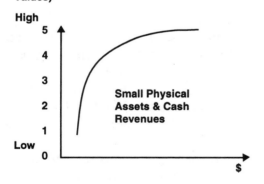

Expenditure Functions:

SCALE   <$50,000   = 1
         $50,000 - $100,000   = 2
         $100,000 - $500,000 = 3
         $500,000 - $1 Million = 4
         >$1 Million   = 5

Linear Scale (Risk Proportionate to Value)

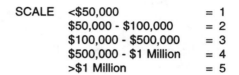
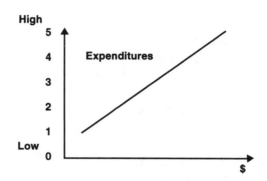

The special case for Risk Factor "Turnover of Key Personnel" (Historical)

SCALE   Moderate Rate 5%/Yr   = 1
         Low/Moderate 2%-5%/Yr = 2
         High/Moderate 5%-8%/Yr = 3
         Low <2%/Yr   = 4
         High >8%/Yr   = 5

U-Shaped (Both Low and High Values are High Risk)

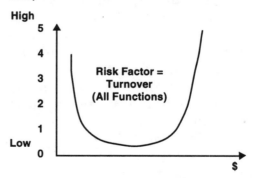

Exercise: Measuring and Classifying Risk

> The purpose of this exercise is to gain experience in measuring and classifying risk.

Background

The National Bank has branches all over the country. Each branch is managed as a separate entity with the ability to hire and fire employees, receive deposits and make loans within their capital limits, and spend money within their budgets. The head office handles national issues, grants loans greater than branch limits, approves branch budgets, selects branch senior management teams, and approves requests for expenses exceeding budgeted amounts. Branches are operated with a set of standard procedures issued by the head office.

Head office auditors visit each branch on a rotating schedule depending on the result of the prior audit:

- Significant adverse or repeat findings: Audit every eight months.
- Small adverse findings: Audit every 12 months.
- No adverse findings: Audit every 16 months.

The audit program for the loan department in each branch lists the following sources of risk and corresponding controls (partial list):

1. *Source of Risk:* Insider loan activity. Loans that are made to employees, directors, or close associates must be handled at arm's length without favoritism.

   Controls:

   - Only loans secured by real or personal property are allowed.

- Bank employee loans are reported to headquarters.
- Bank officers' and directors' loans may only be approved by headquarters.
- Bank officers and directors must file annual financial disclosure statements listing all assets and liabilities, including deposits and loans at the National Bank.

2. *Source of Risk:* Collateral verification. Loan collateral that is pledged must be verified as to ownership, value, and encumbrances.

   Controls:

   - All collateralized loans must have a full description of the collateral, including independent proof of ownership, value, and encumbrances.
   - The verification and custody of collateral should be done by employees who do not make loans to customers.

3. *Source of Risk:* Maintenance of collateral values. Collateral that is pledged may fluctuate in value, deteriorate, or be released prematurely.

   Controls:

   - All collateral held by the bank should be in a negotiable form. Pledged stocks, bonds, deposits, or other instruments should include proper forms signed by the customer that make these instruments negotiable in the event of default by the customer.

   - All collateral should be revalued periodically. Depending on market conditions and type of collateral, this could be monthly, quarterly, or annually.

   - Negotiable collateral is kept in a vault, and all collateral should be released only by a senior loan officer.

4. *Source of Risk:* Repayments. Payment histories must be kept current and proper steps taken to ensure that the loans are repaid.

   Controls:

   - Payments are posted promptly, and an aging of accounts receivable is prepared monthly and approved by the senior loan officer.

   - Strict adherence to loan covenants and default procedures ensures timely foreclosure and other legal remedies to seek repayment.

   - Loans to employees and officers are set up for repayment by payroll deduction (personal property) or automatic debits from their checking accounts (real property).

Data on these risks for the Northeast Branch are as follows:

1. Insider Loans:

   There are 14 loans to 11 individuals with an aggregate value of $840,000.

2. Collateral Verification:

   In the past 12 months, 320 loan applications over $10,000 were received and all involved collateral (personal or real property); 290 were approved for a total of $109,000,000. Simplified loans of less than $10,000 against pledged Certificate of Deposits represented another 415 loans (all approved) for an additional $2,884,000. There were 93 short-term loans approved of less than $5,000 last year that were unsecured for a total of $246,000.

   Total loans outstanding and collateral values as of the end of last quarter:

Total Loans	430,540,000	Total Collateral Values	390,980,000
Personal Property	4,872,000	Collateral Value	4,030,000
Real Property	424,600,000	Collateral Value	386,950,000
Signature Loans	1,068,000	Collateral Value	-0-

3. Collateral types are as follows:

Total Collateral	390,980,000	Real Property	366,950,000
		Securities	20,440,000
		Pledged CDs	2,300,000
		Personal Property	1,290,000

4. Repayments by loan type:

Real Property	97.2% current-90 days	2.8% over 90 days
Personal Property	91.5% current-90 days	8.5% over 90 days
Signature Loans	98.7% current-90 days	1.3% over 90 days

In the past year, 17 foreclosures/forfeitures were processed, representing 0.8% of the loan portfolio value.

Other information:

It has been a tough economic year, with real estate prices flat-to-lower, stock prices off sharply, and interest rates soaring 200 basis points. Earnings at the bank were below projections, and year-end bonuses were withheld from most branches, including the Northeast Branch. The past audit of the Northeast Branch was without significant adverse findings.

Required

In your teams:

Given the four categories of risk, the controls usually relied upon, the prior audit findings, the environment, and the operating data:

1. Develop a method for measuring and classifying these four risks into Low, Medium, or High Risk areas. Be able to justify your reasons for the classification. Use the format that follows.

2. Given a budget of 40 hours of fieldwork, how would you allocate your time among these four areas?

    HINT: Build your "yardstick" first; i.e., what is considered "HIGH" risk, etc.?

    NOTE: This is only a partial list of Sources of Risk and Controls as part of a branch audit.

National Bank Northeast Branch Risk Classification

A.   **Risk**   **Classification**   **Why?**

1. Loans to insiders

2. Collateral verification

3. Collateral maintenance

4. Repayments

B. Budget Allocation in Hours: **Reasons:**

    1. Insider Loans: _____

    2. Collateral Verification: _____

    3. Collateral Maintenance: _____

    4. Repayments: _____

Weighted Matrices

One of the most effective approaches to measuring risk is the use of weighted matrices. Using weighted matrices is similar to using risk factors in that the weighted matrices approach uses auditable unit **components**, and it **weights** certain factors. The differences are in the format (matrices), the risks are somewhat pre-defined, and the process looks at risks over multiple time dimensions.

How this works:

1. The security review, systems design control review, or audit starts with a blank matrix. The left side of the matrix contains a list of the unit's components, and the top of the matrix contains threats. This approach was first described by Dr. Jerry FitzGerald in 1978. It was modified and expanded by David McNamee in 1982 to feature a strategic approach (three dimensions of time).

   a. For current system threats, the weighted matrix approach specifies the risks to the system in the current period as:

      • Errors.
      • Omissions.
      • Delays.
      • Fraud.

   For all components and threats, the matrix can be infinitely expanded to cover specific types of errors, multiple kinds of the same component, different kinds of frauds — whatever deserves specific attention.

   Example: In setting up a threat matrix for cashiering, it would be useful to set up two classes of frauds (cashier theft, customer theft/robbery) as well as several kinds of errors and omissions (wrong account posted, wrong amount disbursed, etc.). In the short-term analysis, we only deal with negative risk and threats, because there is no time to consider opportunities in the short-run.

   b. For mid-term threats and opportunities, the choices are open to those things that could affect profitability or programs in the mid-term, both negatively and positively.

   Example: For many operations, threats in mid-term might include service disruption and waste. Opportunities might include cost avoidance and cost reduction. The issue in the mid-term is on a mix of both negative threats to the process and positive opportunities to contribute to organizational goals and objectives.

   c. For long-term opportunities, the list is usually taken from the business plan or other unit documentation (mission, purpose statement, vision, etc.).

   Example: Most often the statement will include things like customer service, product excellence, quality, leadership, etc. The point is to audit the function to see how the various components help achieve these long-term objectives. In the long-term analysis, we only deal with opportunities and the controls to detect and promote them.

2. Weight the matrices according to the emphasis of the organization on meeting business goals. If the auditor is only concerned about the current state of affairs, the analysis can be limited to a single matrix (in which case this step is skipped).

Example: Common default values for the weighted matrices are:

- Short Term = 65%   This recognizes that much of the negative aspects of risk can affect the organization right away.

- Mid-Term = 25%.   A significant amount of both risk and opportunity exists in operations that are two or three accounting cycles beyond the current period.

- Long Term = 10%.   The organization has to be making progress here, too.

3. As in the Risk Factors approach, weight the threats and opportunities in each matrix as to their importance to preventing/ achieving the organizational goals and objectives. Each matrix is treated separately, so the weights should add to 1.00 for each matrix.

4. Using either a Delphi Group or collaborating with the audit customer, score each of the components for the strength or weakness of the threat or opportunity. The scores are entered into the cell intersections of component vs. threat/opportunity. How are these components affected? Use a scale of 1-to-5, or similar, to express low-to-high exposure.

5. Multiply the scores times the weights of the threats/opportunities. This creates a matrix (spreadsheet) of scaled weighted values.

6. Sum the scaled weighted values for each component across each matrix.

Example: For the Short-Term matrix, sum the scaled weighted values for each component by adding the values for Errors, Omissions, Delays, and Frauds to get a Total Short-Term Value. If the auditor is

only doing a single dimensional risk analysis, this is the final measurement of risks. If using the strategic approach to measure risk across all time dimensions, continue:

7. Make a summary matrix of the three matrices (Short-, Mid-, and Long-Term) across the top and the components along the side. Multiply the raw scaled and weighted values for each cell times the matrix weighing established in step #2.

8. Add the three matrix-weighted scaled values together for a final score. The components with the highest scores are more risky.

Weighted Matrices: A Case Study

The following case study is fully worked out to demonstrate the risk measurement process that uses weighted matrices. The case is an audit of the payroll process.

EXAMPLE PROBLEM:

Rank the following components of the Payroll Process

- Time Reporting Procedures (T/R).
- Deductions and Remittances Position (D & R).
- Payroll Processing Software (PP).
- Check Printing and Distribution Function (P & D).
- Payroll Account Classification (A/C).

Short-Term Financial Risk is weighted 0.65 overall.

Short-Term Threats include:

- F1: Errors   Weight 0.40
- F2: Omissions   Weight 0.25
- F3: Delays   Weight 0.15
- F4: Internal Fraud   Weight 0.10
- F5: External Fraud Weight 0.10

Mid-Term Profitability Risk is weighted 0.25 overall.

Profitability Threats/Opportunities include:

- P1: Cost Savings   Weight 0.60
  Potential
- P2: Cost Avoidance   Weight 0.40
  Potential

Long-Term Improvement Risk is weighted 0.10 overall.

System Improvement Opportunities include:

- I1: Extent of Manual Process   Weight 0.50
- I2: Age of System   Weight 0.30
- I3: Training of Employees   Weight 0.20

Each of the factors was subjectively assessed by a Delphi Group, made up of two members of the audit team and two members from the payroll unit. The assessments were in a range of 1-10, with 1 being lowest risk impact and 10 the highest risk impact. These assessments were then multiplied by the subjectively assigned weights (also using a Delphi Group technique based on years of prior knowledge).

EXAMPLE PROBLEM

STEP 1: ASSIGN SUBJECTIVE ASSESSMENTS 1 (LOW) 10 (HIGH)

RISK FACTORS AND WEIGHTS

UNIT COMP.	F1 0.40	F2 0.25	F3 0.15	F4 0.10	F5 0.10	P1 0.60	P2 0.40	I1 0.50	I2 0.30	I3 0.20
T/R	4	5	3	4	3	2	6	6	3	4
D & R	5	6	6	4	3	5	2	4	5	3
PP	3	7	4	6	5	3	7	5	5	5
P & D	5	4	7	5	3	3	7	7	2	6
A/C	3	4	7	5	5	1	5	3	2	3

Each of the Auditable Units has been assessed its rating on a scale of 1 (low) to 10 (high) for each of the Risk Factors in the model. At this stage of the problem, each of the auditable units in turn have strengths and weaknesses that make it difficult to assign audit priority just by looking at the factor scores. Not all risk factors have equal weights, either in this problem or in reality.

The next steps apply the weights of each factor to their factor assessment score.

STEP 2: DERIVE SCALED VALUES (MULTIPLY ASSESSMENTS * WEIGHTS)

RISK FACTORS AND WEIGHTS

UNIT COMP.	F1 0.40	F2 0.25	F3 0.15	F4 0.10	F5 0.10	P1 0.60	P2 0.40	I1 0.50	I2 0.30	I3 0.20
T/R	1.6	1.3	0.5	0.4	0.3	1.2	2.4	3.0	0.9	0.8
D & R	2.0	1.5	0.9	0.4	0.3	3.0	0.8	2.0	1.5	0.6
PP	1.2	1.8	0.6	0.6	0.5	1.8	2.8	2.5	1.5	1.0
P & D	2.0	1.0	1.1	0.5	0.3	1.8	2.8	3.5	0.6	1.2
A/C	1.2	1.0	1.1	0.5	0.5	0.6	2.0	1.5	0.6	0.6

The values thus derived represent the weighted value of each factor. The weighing of the factors gives a relative importance to each. That has the effect of smoothing out some of the effects of high raw scores in areas of lesser importance. The high scores in less important areas are dampened by the low relative weighing.

The final two steps are to sum the factors in each dimension for a raw score and then apply the Dimension Weight of each matrix to the sum; the dimension weighted values are then summed for a Total Assessment Score.

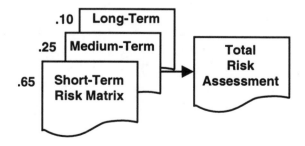

EXAMPLE PROBLEM (CONTINUED):

STEP 3: SUM WEIGHTED ASSESSMENTS FOR EACH FACTOR AND DIMENSION

STEP 4: APPLY DIMENSION WEIGHTS TO SUMS

UNIT COMP.	SHORT-TERM FINANCIAL WEIGHT = .65 RAW	WTD	/RANK	MID-TERM PROFITABILITY WEIGHT = .25 RAW	WTD	LONG-TERM IMPROVEMENT WEIGHT = .10 RAW	WTD	TOTAL ASSESSMENT SCORE	/RANK
T/R	4.0	2.6	5	3.6	0.9	4.4	0.4	3.9	4
D & R	5.1	3.3	1	3.8	1.0	4.1	0.4	4.7	3
PP	4.7	3.1	3	4.6	1.2	4.6	0.5	4.8	2
P & D	4.9	3.2	2	4.6	1.2	4.8	0.5	4.9	1
A/C	4.3	2.8	4	2.6	0.7	3.1	0.3	3.8	5

The Financial Dimension represents immediate risk, the Profitability Dimension represents medium term risk and reward, and the Improvement Dimension represents long-term gains and risks. In our example, the area where testing would have been more extensive using only Financial Risk Factors would have been Deductions & Remittances with a score of 5.1. However, when the other dimensions are included and Financial is weighted to 65% of the total, Deductions & Remittances slips down to third place, and Check Printing & Distribution and Payroll Processing Software move up to first and second respectively.

CHAPTER 7
RISK PRIORITIZATION

The final step in business risk assessment is to prioritize (or rank) the risks (or more accurately, prioritize the organization or unit's components according to risks and consequences) so that risk-based decisions can be made. Risk measurement is the larger and more difficult task. Prioritizing the risks after measuring them requires little extra effort. The purpose of ranking or prioritizing risk is the same as the purpose for risk assessment itself: *To make decisions about applying relative effort to various components of the organization/unit/project based on the relative strength of risks and consequences each component faces.*

There are three methods to prioritize risks:

- **Absolute Ranking:** The risks and consequences to the components or elements of the auditable unit are identified and measured. The components are ranked by their score.

- **Relative Ranking:** The risks and consequences to the components or elements of the auditable unit are identified and measured. The scores are grouped into natural clusters (breaks in sequence)

and assigned relative values such as Low, Medium, or High.

- **Matrices Ranking:** This is a form of relative ranking that manipulates the matrices that were used to measure the risks and consequences to the components or elements of the auditable unit. By sorting the axes from their joining point, quadrants of High, Medium, and Low can be identified.

Absolute Ranking

Absolute ranking takes the output (scores, measures, etc.) from risk measurement and places the output in order of magnitude. This can be accomplished with a number of similar algorithms:

1. **Total Score:** The total scores are ranked in order of magnitude.

Example: The Annual Loss Expectancy for each component in the data center has been measured for all material risks and consequences, and the results are:

Asset (Component)	Annualized Loss Expectancy *ALE*	Rank
CPU	960	1
DASD	900	2
Tape Drives	360	3/4
Printers	360	3/4
Console	80	5
TOTAL	2,660	

The prudent auditor would design an audit program that balanced the hours to these projected consequences: more hours to reviewing the controls protecting the CPU than reviewing the controls protecting the DASD, and so on for the other components.

2. **Proportional Ranking:** The components' total scores are converted into a percentage of the sum of all scores. This is useful for spreading an audit budget over the unit's components.

    Example: In our table above, the CPU represents 36% *(960/2,660)*, the DASD 34%, Tape Drives and Printers each 14%, and the Console 2%. A fieldwork budget of 40

hours could be distributed by using these percentages. As a practical matter, we would ignore the Console.

3. **Average Ranking:** The components' total scores are converted to an average risk score by dividing the total by the number of risk factors before ranking in order of magnitude. This is not a common method, as it adds no real value to the planning decision.

    Example: The auditor identified five risk factors in the auditable unit, and the unit's components were scored on the strength and presence of each of the five factors. The scores were averaged over the five factors before ranking.[1]

Component	F1	F2	F3	F4	F5	Total Score	Average	Rank
T/R	1.6	1.3	0.5	0.4	0.3	4.1	0.82	4
D & R	2.0	1.5	0.9	0.4	0.3	5.1	1.02	1
PP	1.2	1.8	0.6	0.6	0.5	3.7	0.74	5
P & D	2.0	1.0	1.1	0.5	0.3	4.9	0.98	2
A/C	1.2	1.0	1.1	0.5	0.5	4.3	0.86	3

A variation of the average ranking algorithm is to divide the total scores by some other arbitrary value. If this results in the scores being normalized to sum to 1.00, then the ranking process is identical to Proportional Ranking (number 2, above).

---

[1]Mathematically, the ranking is identical to total score rank because each score is divided by the same number — average scores may be used for other reasons. See for example, Ziegenfuss, Douglas E, *Challenges and Opportunities of Small Internal Auditing Organizations* (Altamonte Springs, FL: The Institute of Internal Auditors Research Foundation, 1994), p. 78.

Relative Ranking

Relative ranking only seeks to classify the components of the auditable unit into broad risk classifications, such as Low, Medium, and High. This is often sufficient for general planning purposes; however, this method does not provide the same audit budgeting assistance that Proportional Ranking offers. Relative ranking can be developed by direct calculation, pattern matching, or normative tables:

1. **Direct Calculation:** The components' total risk scores are calculated and then grouped, either by pre-defined ranges or by "cluster ranges."

    a. Pre-defined ranges are score ranges that are set up in advance, such as <20 = Low, 20 to 39 = Medium, 40+ = High Risk. Pre-defined ranges, if they can be validated over time, are useful for comparing one audit with another.

    b. Cluster ranges are not strictly pre-defined. Instead, the values are examined for **natural gaps**, and the clusters are labeled Low, Medium, or High. Many university professors rank student grades by this approach, also known as "gap-osis."

    Example: For a set of scores, define the values based on natural gaps in the sequence:

HIGH		MEDIUM				LOW
56	<u>51</u>	42	<u>36</u>	21	19	11

2. **Pattern Matching:** Instead of basing the component's rank on the total risk score (sum of risk factors), the scores of each factor are significant, and the pattern determines the overall risk classification. Usually, the difference in significance or consequences of different risk factors are handled by weighting the factors. Two conditions may make this approach important:

    a. Fraud. In some situations, especially when fraud is a concern, the risk of fraud becomes an overriding factor. Certain "red flags" can influence the extent and type of audit effort.

    b. Sparse distribution of factors. If risk factors are not common among auditable units because of the variety of units in the audit plan, certain risks may be not applicable to some components but are applicable to others. If the matrix is sparse, the total scores are not valid measures of risk and cannot be effectively used in ranking.

Example: The following risk measurement matrix of an operational audit of a training department is an example of a **sparse matrix**. *The auditor should prioritize the audit components based on analysis of the patterns of each scored factor (Low = 1, High = 5):*

Component	Factor 1: Contribution to Profits	Factor 2: Contribution to Image	Factor 3: Contribution to Employees	Factor 4: Contribution to Goals
Training Materials	2	2	3	N/A
Training Facilities	4	3	N/A	N/A
Audio Visual Equipment	3	N/A	1	N/A
Trainers	5	4	5	3
Supervision Leadership	5	1	3	5
Budget	4	N/A	3	3
Quality Assurance Processes	2	2	3	4

3. **Normative Tables:** The components' risks are not measured numerically; instead, the risks are classified using a descriptive model. The measurement table usually includes descriptions of risk and controls and the combinations of risks and controls equate to levels of concern.

Matrices Ranking

Matrices ranking was developed by Jerry FitzGerald. Using a matrix of threats or risk along the top and the unit's components along the left side, a risk matrix is developed. The completed matrix is ranked by the following procedure:

1. Using a Delphi team, perform comparison risk ranking of the threats and a comparison risk ranking of the components. The ranking is ordinal; i.e., the items are listed in order of preference and not numerically evaluated.

2. Rearrange the matrix with axes flowing from highest to lowest scores, starting at the upper left corner (highest threat vs. most important component). The least threat and the least important component (lowest scores in each) will be at the bottom right corner. Place the scores of each threat-component pair in their cell and divide the scores into quartiles on the chart with a line marking the boundary of the cells with the highest 25% of the scores and another outlining the lowest 25% of the scores.

3. The risk assessment can be made directly from the final risk-ranked matrix of threats, components and cells (controls): the cell scores in the upper quartile represent HIGH RISK, the scores in the lowest quartile represent LOW RISK, and the scores of the middle two quartiles define MEDIUM RISK.

   Example: Assuming that the axes of the following matrix are now sorted from highest to lowest importance (Errors and Omissions and On-Line Terminals are HIGHEST, Physical Disasters and Operating Procedures are LOWEST), the matrix is ranked by quartiles:

HINT: To more easily rank order a list, using a "paired ranking" technique can be helpful. This technique involves choosing opposite pairs among those remaining on the list. The technique starts with choosing the BEST item and WORST item, placing them FIRST and LAST respectively. The next and subsequent steps repeat the process, choosing from the list the NEXT BEST and NEXT WORST items, and so forth.

"X" APPLICATION SYSTEM

THREATS ⟋ COMPO-NENTS	ERRORS and OMISSIONS	BREACH of PRIVACY	ILLEGAL ACCESS	THEFT	LOST DATA	PHYSICAL DISASTERS
ONLINE TERMINALS	H	H	H	M	M	M
TERMINAL OPERATORS	H	H	H	M	M	M
SOFTWARE PROGRAMS	H	H	M	M	L	L
DATA FILES	M	M	M	L	L	L
OPERATING PROCEDURES	M	M	L	L	L	L

H = HIGH RISK

M = MEDIUM RISK

L = LOW RISK

The audit program would concentrate more testing for threat-component pairs that rank HIGH and less for those ranked LOW.

Exercise: Risk Assessment Case Study

The purpose of this part of the exercise is to gain experience in identifying risk through brainstorming in an information systems context.

Background

The data center is the main information system asset in this organization. There are also a large number of personal computers spread throughout the organization; however, the main dollar assets are in the central computer center. The center houses two IBM 3090 mainframes, 24 large capacity DASD devices (disk drives), several tape drives, printers, and assorted controllers and front end processors. There is a large amount of telecommunications gear and a large modem pool to serve the 200+ users that dialed into the data center for e-mail and other telecommunications applications.

The data center is located in the basement of the main office tower. It is accessible only through locked doors controlled by magnetic identification cards and manned by uniformed guards. The center is staffed 24 hours a day and seven days a week. Preventative maintenance and production tuning is conducted from midnight Saturday to 0800 Sunday. During the maintenance period, the data center is unavailable.

Backing up the data center power supply is a UPS (uninterruptible power supply) system which included a battery room in the basement with power for 20 minutes and a diesel generator on the roof to recharge the batteries. Commercial city power is fed through the battery packs to keep them continuously charged and to "clean" the commercial power of spikes and slumps in power delivery. The computer room is cooled by three high capacity air conditioners and one spare. The CPUs are water cooled and served by a reciprocating pump in the basement with a reservoir tank and heat exchanger.

Fire suppression includes hand operated CO_2 extinguishers, a Halon gas system, smoke and heat sensors, and manual and automatic alarms. Tarps are available for fire suppression or water protection.

Data protection includes a standard "log tape" that is part of the back up and recovery system. Data, programs, and documentation are archived regularly and sent to off-site secure storage by a third-party service contractor. Logical security is maintained through user passwords that are changed every six months. Program security includes industry standard change control procedures and a separation of application testing from system development activities.

Disaster recovery procedures are available, including step-by-step instructions on major disasters. The procedures include a "call-out" list of managers that should be notified in case of a major catastrophe. Disaster drills are scheduled every year.

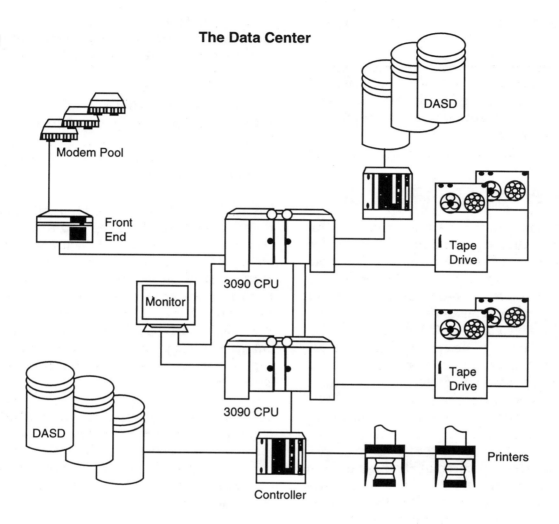

The Data Center

Required

In your teams, brainstorm to develop a list of threats to the reliability and security of the data center. Brainstorm rules are found on the next page. Reduce your list to the 8 most significant threats (most likely and most impact).

Brainstorming Rules

SET UP: Use a blackboard/whiteboard or easel with chart paper. Everyone must be able to see at once. The easel is preferred because of the limited space on a board.

Appoint a scribe to work at the board or easel. The scribe may also act as the leader, if desired.

1. The leader sets up the question to be answered. It is best to write it on the easel.

2. The leader sets the time limit for input (10 minutes to 30 minutes is usually more than enough).

3. The leader explains the rules of participation:

    a. Each person can contribute as much as they want
    b. No comments, criticisms, or judgments are allowed during the storming phase
    c. It is okay to build on others ideas (it is actually encouraged)
    d. The storming phase is over at the time limit or when all ideas have been exhausted.

4. At the "go" signal, each person begins to suggest an answer. The scribe must capture each answer as given without editing (abbreviation is okay). The scribe may enforce some order on the suggestors if the scribe has trouble capturing the suggestions (one-at-a-time, raise hands, etc. — most sessions don't need these).

5. When all suggestions have been offered or the time has expired, the leader will attempt to consolidate similar suggestions (with permission of the group) for ease in later selection or prioritization.

Data Center Risk Identification

Threats   Why?

1.

2.

3.

4.

5.

6.

7.

8.

Other Threats (Optional):

Exercise: Risk Assessment Case Study (Continued)

> **The purpose of this part of the exercise is to gain experience in using matrices for measuring risk.**

Background

This is a continuation of the data center risk assessment case.

Required

Using the diagram and the narrative from the first part of the exercise, identify the six most important components of the data center. To assist you, the following are some of the components that contribute to data center reliability and security:

- Hardware: CPUs, Controllers, Printers, Tape Drives, DASD, Monitor

- Telecommunications: Front End, Modem Pool

- Software: Operating System, Applications, Backup & Recovery

- People: Computer Operators, Supervisors, Managers, Guards

- Physical Protection: Locked Doors, Alarm System, Halon System, Other Fire Protection Equipment

- HVAC and Power: Air Conditioning, Water Cooling, Power, UPS Batteries, Diesel Generator

- Procedures and Policies: Disaster Recovery, Run Documentation, Security Policies, Preventative Maintenance, Backup & Recovery, Offsite Storage, Program Change Controls, Separation of Duties, Disaster Drills

Example: You may choose to measure risk on individual components or groups of components or a combination of both. For example, your six most important components might be: CPU, Locked Doors, Alarm System, Guards, UPS, Policies and Procedures. The first five were individual components, and the last was an entire group.

Data Center Component Identification

Important Component   **Why?**

1.

2.

3.

4.

5.

6.

7.

8.

Other Important Components (Optional):

Exercise: Risk Assessment Case Study (Continued)

> The purpose of this final part of the exercise is to gain experience in using weighted matrices to rank Threat/Component cells as well as evaluating internal control strength in audit planning.

Background

> This is the final part of the data center risk assessment case.

Required

In your teams, consensus rank both the threats and the components you identified in the earlier parts of this exercises and place them on the matrix on the following page in order of importance from HIGHEST to LOWEST starting at the upper left corner. Place a **W** in the intersecting squares to represent your assessment of control strength as **Weak**, place an **S** if you think controls are reasonably **Strong**, or leave **Blank** if there are no controls or no evidence in the narrative for that threat on that component.

Example: If you have **Fire** as a threat and **CPU** as a component, do you rate the controls over Fire that protect the CPU as Weak, Strong, or None? Examine the earlier narrative for the exercise for clues.

The result of the above effort is a weighted matrix with a preliminary audit program established showing what are the most important areas to audit based on an assessment of risk. The extent and type of audit testing can be determined by examining the number and strength of controls in each area.

Threats / Components	1	2	3	4	5	6	7	8

CHAPTER 8
RISK MODEL IMPLEMENTATION

There are many ways to approach business risk assessment, from ignoring the risk to using scientific mathematical models, and many ways in between. The following recommendations are based on the experiences of many people:

1. The risk assessment process must produce *credible* results that are accepted by management.

2. The risk assessment process must be *timely* so that the planning process is not held back waiting for results.

3. The risk assessment process must be *cost-effective* in that the resulting information is at least as valuable as the cost to obtain it.

4. Computers can help make the assessment process faster by handling data and calculations, but *the key to successful risk assessment is in understanding and identifying risk.*

5. Use intuition as a check for all risk assessments. The assessment must "make sense" to an experienced manager.

6. Scale your risk assessment process or model to the resources and needs of your organization. Simplify as much as possible.

7. Involve your senior management and external auditor in the process early. If they need to have comfort, and you may need to synchronize your approach and assumptions with an assessment process already in place.

8. Risk models are not necessary to perform risk assessment; however, models have advantages over performing an original approach each time:

- Models make risk assessment easier to explain to others.
- Models help maintain consistency in assessments.
- Models can be used to train others about risk assessment.

9. Involve the end user in risk assessment.

Macro and Micro Risk Assessment Models

Business risk assessment is effective at two levels:

1. Macro planning: The strategic planning model uses risk assessment to sort out the major issues to be addressed. Internal auditing macro risk assessment is used to develop the annual audit plan.

2. Micro planning: The project-planning model uses risk assessment to identify components of the project/unit/audit that need additional attention by local management.

There are models for both, although the models are usually different in some details. The most effective macro models tend to be factor-driven, while the most effective micro models are often matrix models. Both sets of models can be one-dimensional or multidimensional.

The One-Dimensional Model

The most common risk assessment model type is one-dimensional. The risk assessment is performed for the current situation of the enterprise. It is risk assessment using what is known today and what the consequences of risk are on the present. One-dimensional models address only current risks. Rarely are opportunities considered (by their nature, opportunities, are *future* events). Common concerns can be classified as one of four threats: errors, omissions, delays, or fraud.

One-dimensional models are the most common in practice. They are useful for depicting the state of the current decision environment — the forces at work in the present that will cause you to fail to achieve your objectives. Most one-dimensional models can be used on simple spreadsheets, with or without computer assistance.

One-dimensional models are quick to use and relatively simple and easy to explain to others where these are important features. The models can be reasonably accurate predictors of risk, given a good source of information about the current environment. Simplicity is both a strength and a weakness. One-dimensional models are not "real world," and they are limited for strategic planning. These models are more like econometric models that predict outcomes with the caveat "all other things being equal..." These models are favored by analysts because they are easy to construct and operate; however, the results are not reliable over time.

The Two-Dimensional Model

Some authors have advocated that risk analysis should include *profitability* as a second dimension. These two-dimensional models have caught the interest of senior management in for-profit enterprises on the basis of this additional dimension. Two-dimensional models require the risk assessment be completed twice: once for current risk and once for the unit's contribution to profits. The only written source of such a model focuses on auditing for *risk* and *cost savings and recoveries*. Cost savings/recoveries is the measure of profitability in this model. A weighting method (can be equal or different weights) is used to assign a score for both risk and profitability. The scores are summed and the risk assessment completed by ranking the highest total scores.

The two-dimensional model is used by those who have a desire to demonstrate "added value" to the enterprise. It helps balance decisions between current risk and short-term profitability.

The two-dimensional model recognizes that risk is more than what we perceive that could happen in the current time period. It is an effective method for factoring in the contribution to profitability of the unit. Current usage of the model focuses on cost savings/recovery. There are several other major risk/opportunity factors that deal with profitability and effectiveness that are not often used.

The MultiDimensional Model

A new model for risk assessment is proposed. It is a continuous view of the effects of both risk and opportunity over time horizons representing current/short-term financial risk, mid-term risk/opportunities, and long-term risk/opportunities. The main features include:

- The recognition that *Risk* and *Opportunity* are mirror images of the same phenomenon.

- Division of risk into time horizons or *Multiple Dimensions*:
  - Short Term or Current Financial Risk
  - Mid-term (beyond the current accounting period) Risk/Opportunity
  - Long-term Risk/Opportunity.

- Classification of all Current Financial risks into either *Errors*, *Omissions*, *Delays*, or *Frauds*. The explicit recognition of *Opportunities* as another aspect of risk in future events that can be combined with current values of risk.

- Reliance on *Consensus* in building the matrix, and the ability to weight matrices to achieve a weighted action plan that addresses all time horizons simultaneously.

This model can be used for decisions involving risk in project management, portfolio management, and auditing. It closely mirrors the strategic outlook of senior management.

The strengths of the multidimensional approach:

- It more closely approximates management strategic planning processes.
- It fosters consensus management and team-building consistent with the principles of Total Quality Management.

The weaknesses of the multidimensional approach are in its relative complexity. The multidimensional model requires many times more calculations to achieve its results. Because of this, the model is limited generally to micro risk assessment situations where the number of factors or functions is fewer than 15. The pair-wise voting and calculations are too numerous for most macro risk assessment/ranking.

Risk models are an effective way to solve many problems in an efficient and effective manner. The alternative is to treat each risk assessment as a separate problem. Models have a number of common elements that address both macro and micro risk assessment. The two major approaches to macro risk assessment are Direct Assignment of weighted values or using the Analytic Hierarchy Process. Micro risk assessment uses a matrix approach in one-dimensional, two-dimensional, or multidimensional models. The multidimensional approach is by far the best fit with senior management's strategic planning process.

Major Implementation Issues

Prudent management uses risk assessment in strategic (macro) planning and in project/unit/audit (micro) planning. However, building models or purchasing commercial software is an option, because using risk assessment principles does not necessarily mean formally modeling risk.

The major issues for implementation are:

- Making the choice between formal models or not.
- Making the choice between developing your own model or purchasing commercial risk assessment software.
- How to evaluate the model.
- Getting buy-in from users and management.
- Getting buy-in from top management and the external auditor.

If the decision is to forgo the formal model approach, then risk assessment will be undocumented and ad hoc. The auditor may ask a number of people for their opinion on topics of importance (a collegial approach), or the auditor may make his or her own determination of risk.

Many people believe that managerial judgment is superior to formulas and computer programs when it comes to business risk assessment. Quite a few organizations still rely exclusively on judgment; that is, they do not have a formal risk assessment process. How do we determine if we should try to build our own process or buy a commercial computer package? Are there some methods of getting auditor "buy-in" to use the model instead of their own intuition? Are there some methods that we can use with our management clients to get their support and "buy-in" for using a risk assessment model? What are some of the hurdles in gaining the support of the senior management team and the external auditor for using risk assessment models? These are some of the human aspects of risk assessment implementation.

The two criteria for managing a risk assessment project are:

1. The risk project manager must have achieved a lot of respect and trust in the organization.

2. The risk project manager must be skilled in "selling" new ideas to people.

Deciding on the "Make-or-Buy" Question

Deciding to build your own process or to purchase software to perform risk assessment is a difficult decision in many cases.

The advantages of designing and building our own process:

1. The risk factors and the model can be designed to fit our organization, our risk factors and our culture.

2. We can make the process as simple or complex as we want.

3. We can use this project to learn more about risk ourselves and to train junior managers about risk.

4. If we can involve both users and managers on the project team, we will get better acceptance for our ideas of risk (better "buy-in").

The disadvantages of designing and building our own process:

1. It will take time from doing other things.

2. You may not have the skill to handle the project yourself and have to hire a consultant.

3. It may take too long.

4. Your design may be flawed.

For these reasons, many internal audit departments consider commercial software as an important alternative to designing and building their own risk assessment program.

Evaluating Commercial Assessment Software

Risk assessment and risk management require either a lot of data or a lot of computations or both. The handling of such requirements means that most risk models are computerized. The software is one of three types:

- Developed by the user using a programming language.

  It is uncommon, except for some of the largest organizations, to attempt to develop a risk assessment process using a software programming language. This approach is avoided by most because so few users are also software programmers. Occasionally this approach is taken when there are special circumstances or as part of a larger administrative project. The critical success factors are understanding the language and understanding risk and how to assess it.

- Developed by the user using a standard software package (spreadsheet or database or both).

  The most common approach is for the user to develop a risk assessment process based around a commercially developed spreadsheet, database, or both. The process can be reasonably customized, and the development skills and time required are significantly less than using a programming language. The critical knowledge is understanding what risk is and how to identify, measure, and prioritize risk.

- Purchased by the user (specialized commercial risk assessment software developed from a programming language or based on a commercial spreadsheet, database, or both).

  Commercial risk assessment software for personal computers have been on the market for at least 10 years, either as special assessment programs, add-in modules to spreadsheet programs, or as part of a larger program package. Even external audit firms are in the marketplace with risk assessment software.

Using commercial risk assessment software has several advantages over building the software yourself. There are also some disadvantages to consider before purchasing a commercial package. There are many commercial versions of risk assessment software on the market, so it is best to approach them with a consistent method of evaluating your needs and their features and capabilities.

The key advantages for selecting a commercial risk assessment software package include minimal development effort, low cost in relation to building the same process yourself, tested and documented algorithms, software user groups, periodic upgrades, and user support.

Developing your own software, or even creating your own spreadsheet file, can be time-consuming. Commercial software is usually a matter of "load-and-go." The development time is minimal, usually just to read the operations manual and to establish your own default values. Costs to purchase the software are often only a fraction of the cost to reproduce the software yourself. The costs may appear to be high in relation to developing a small spreadsheet application, but the other advantages are worth the investment.

The software in commercial risk assessment packages has been thoroughly tested and documented, which most do-it-yourself spreadsheets and databases are not. The added assurance of this level of testing and documentation is one of the key advantages of commercial software.

Many software vendors have affiliated user groups that are a source of new ideas for using the software and for possible upgrades. A software user group also gives you another level of support for problem solving. Software vendors will be constantly seeking ways to improve the product to meet the changing needs of customers and the changes in the computer environment. Most homegrown software is built and then rarely upgraded. Software vendors also supply extended user support. Most locally developed software depends on a single individual's knowledge and availability to offer support. The common cause of failure for locally developed programs is the absence of the program's designer.

Although there are many advantages to commercially developed software over locally developed software, there are also some disadvantages. The most common problem is that the developer's product does not meet 100% of your needs (which you should be able to get with a custom product). Other issues that have been raised include the difficulty in managing the software, inflexibility, and the cost of upgrades.

A few software vendors can customize their product superficially to meet your needs — usually producing customized reports that have been reformatted to fit with your administrative system. Most cannot do even that, and none can modify their basic approach to meet a perceived client need. Even with those that offer some customizing, the cost is quite high.

The basic rule is: if the package meets most of your needs, it is usually best to adopt or reject the package rather than pay to have it altered.

Some program packages require a great deal of data gathering and data manipulation before they can be operated. They usually cannot run with skeleton records, so a lot of effort is expended gathering the data and keeping it current. If your operation changes often, this can be burdensome.

Software packages that attempt to deal with a narrow business problem like risk assessment naturally must choose among the common approaches to risk assessment. This act of choice means that the program is usually not flexible to be used for something else. The more generic a program is, the easier it is to use for other applications (electronic spreadsheets, for example); however, these programs require a lot of user effort for each application.

The cost of upgrades and support can be considerable. For large staffs, if everyone is using the software, it can be an expensive situation. One strategy for upgrades is to skip every other issue. Microsoft has stated that they intend to make a minor upgrade even other year and a major upgrade in the intervening years. Some software vendors are becoming more sensitive to the upgrade issue, and they are making substantial concessions to site licensees and bulk purchasers.

Commercial software has many advantages over do-it-yourself programming or simple homegrown spreadsheet/database models. Commercial software is usually tested and documented to much higher standards than custom-built software, and there are added advantages of periodic upgrades, user groups and third party support. The biggest drawback to commercial software is the inability to customize and adapt the program beyond certain superficial items. Thus, if the program meets your needs, it is definitely a best buy over trying to develop your own program. If the program does not meet your needs, then it is best not to buy it. The key is assessing each potential purchase using accepted criteria for program structure and program performance in conjunction with your operating environment and probable changes in your organization.

Standard Software Evaluation Criteria

By using a set of standard criteria, a user can establish which among the commercial products best fits the needs of the organization. Two sets of attributes are recommended: structural attributes that describe how the model interfaces with the user, and performance attributes that describe how the model achieves its purpose.

A number of risk assessment packages attempt to add value or differentiate themselves from their competition by including other features such as project planning and project/audit administration. These are largely macro risk assessment models, and they can be a good value if the need for project/audit administration is already high. Standard software evaluation criteria include:

Structural Attributes

Structural attributes have to do with the "look and feel" of the software. Does it do what was expected? Do results make sense? Is the user in control over the software, or vice versa?

1. **Simple:** Structure is well understood. Input is seen to be relevant and concise. Important relationships are included and less important ones left out. Problem assumptions are understood and acceptable to decision makers.

Simple is straightforward, it is not "simplistic." A good software package will be well documented, including flow diagrams and other graphic aids to make the process easily understood.

2. **Robust:** The model does not produce absurd answers and varies in a manner consistent with underlying assumptions.

   Robust means that the software is fault-tolerant or self-correcting. The program can handle a variety or a volume of transactions without degrading or breaking.

3. **Easy to Control and Understand:** Cause-and-effect relationships between inputs and outputs are readily established. It "feels" right and "makes sense."

   Related to simple, easy to control understand means that there are visible controls within the program that allow for viewing intermediate process results. The tasks required to produce the final results make sense in terms of effort and level of detail.

4. **Adaptive:** Model can be updated as the modeled system evolves.

   This attribute relates especially to the ease with which the software handles changes in volumes and restructuring of assessment units. Programs that have a very rigid structure, such as fixed-length fields or fixed limits to number of entries, are not adaptive.

5. **Complete:** The most important phenomena are included in the model.

   The program should have sufficient room to include all relevant risk factors or whatever criteria the user requires. The user must not have to leave out any relevant data or factors.

6. **Easy to Communicate with:** Managers feel involved and believe they 'own' and can work with the approach.

   The software acts as a tool and not the master of the risk assessment process.

Performance Attributes

Risk assessment software can be developed that is more customer focused. The software needs to address risks from management's perspective. Risk models are part of the creative strategic thinking process and provide a good basis for continuous improvement in the operation of the organization. The software we choose must have high performance characteristics.

1. **Quantify risk and opportunity with equal ease**, measuring both against actual system outcomes.

   The software should give the user the means to measure both positive and negative variation in the system.

2. **Provide a means to both reduce risk and improve system performance**.

   The software should give the user an appreciation of where system improvements might be worthwhile, based on the risks and opportunities the system has identified.

3. **Provide an ongoing assessment tool**.

   The software should provide the user with a means to capture and display historical data as well as current risk.

4. **Involve both managers and users of system outcomes in a way that increases "buy-in" from the critical stakeholders**.

Ideally, the software should be a tool that can be used to build consensus about the risk assessment of a particular project. The software should be consistent and logical to facilitate explanation. In addition, the software should allow for capturing multiple views or opinions and combining them into a consensus result.

5. **Use time and resources efficiently**.

The software should produce results with greater than the time and effort needed to produce them.

There are still many audit professionals who do not use any formal approach to risk assessment. With the number of relatively inexpensive commercial programs available for macro and micro risk assessment, there are no excuses for avoiding audit professional standards in this area. Each of the programs reviewed has strong and weak points, and some programs are more suitable for certain sizes of staff and other conditions. Care should be taken to select the program that meets your current and future needs.

Management and User "Buy-In"

It is often the rest of the people in the organization that have the biggest influence on the success of a risk assessment process. If auditors or other users will not use the process, if management clients have no faith in the process outputs, and if senior management and/or the external auditor do not support the process, risk assessment will fail. Besides having a good plan and a good process, successful implementation of risk assessment depends on good people skills in the implementation manager. Many organizations that start a formal risk assessment process later abandon that process in favor of intuition. In studies in the UK and the U.S., approximately one-third of all audit departments still use intuition without any pretext of a formal assessment program.

Another third use intuition but make some sort of spreadsheet or listing to give the process some regularity. Only about one-third use a true risk assessment model process.

Building or buying sophisticated tools will not produce a risk assessment process. We still need these tools to be effectively used in order to achieve our objectives. In any change management process, we need to be sure that the people who must change (the users of the risk assessment process, such as the auditors) will embrace the change. This process of "buy-in" is very important to the implementation. Otherwise the risk assessment tools will go unused and the investment in time and effort will be wasted.

Involve the users:

1. Solicit opinions from users about the need for a change in methods.

2. Appoint users to the project team to design and/or select the risk assessment process to be used.

3. Train some "early adopters" — those users that enjoy exploring new ideas and working with new tools. These users can be models and serve to do peer-to-peer training for the rest.

4. Use the suggestions of the users to upgrade the process.

Educate the users:

1. Involve users in education programs or seminar about risk assessment.

2. Link risk assessment with important individual and/or group goals, such as efficiency, effectiveness, customer satisfaction and quality, and professionalism.

3. Circulate success stories and articles from the professional literature demonstrating the usefulness of risk assessment.

Risk assessment practitioners should use many of the same techniques for gaining the support of our customers as they did for other users. Our customers are just as much users as our own staff, because risk assessment is performed *on behalf of* our customers, even though it is our staff that actually does most of the assessing. Both our people and our customers have a large stake in the outcome of the assessment.

Involve the customers:

1. Solicit opinions from customers about the need for a change in methods.

2. Appoint customers to the project team to design and/or select the risk assessment process to be used.

3. Convince some "early adopters" — those customers that enjoy exploring new ideas and working with new tools. These customers can be models for the rest.

4. Use the suggestions of the customers to upgrade the process.

Educate the customers:

1. Involve customers in education programs or seminar about risk assessment.

2. Link risk assessment with important individual and/or group goals, such as efficiency, effectiveness, quality management, and professionalism.

3. Circulate success stories and articles from the professional literature demonstrating the usefulness of risk assessment.

A business risk assessment process is a major strategic tool and can be a competitive advantage in itself. As such, implementing a business risk assessment process should have the backing of all major stakeholders, including the senior management team and the external auditor or regulatory agency.

Special concerns:

1. Senior management may not understand the need or even understand risk assessment itself.

2. Senior management and/or the external auditor may be using a risk assessment process already. There may be a need to synchronize the models into a consistent view of the exposures.

3. There may be serious concerns that implementation will be expensive.

4. There may be a feeling of relinquishing control "to some formula."

Senior management's concerns:

1. We may need to educate management as we would educate the users and direct customers of the process.

2. Synchronization or reconciliation of assumptions is an important task.

3. Efficiency may have to be demonstrated by using a pilot study or other limited implementation (or using case histories of other organizations).

4. You may need to involve senior management in enough depth to assure them of maintaining control over their destiny. One method that has been helpful is to add an "audit step" in the business risk assessment process by asking: ***Does this outcome make sense?***

Implementing business risk assessment is not easy. Such a project involves people, and each person has their own ideas about the nature of risk and about the nature of change. We need to anticipate the resistance to change and build in positive controls that enable us to implement risk assessment successfully. Risk assessment is a process tool. Process tools are generally hard to explain — they need to be experienced. The key to successful implementation is to get all levels in the organization and all stakeholders to get some experience of the process through helping design or test the process.

CHAPTER 9
RISK MANAGEMENT

Risk management includes risk assessment and the process of acting on that assessment. Using risk assessment in the planning stages assumes (rightly or wrongly) that prudent management will take the necessary steps to manage the risk once it is assessed. Risk assessment includes a three-step process:

1. Risk Identification: Understanding what the risks and consequences of those risks can be.

2. Risk Measurement: Measuring the likely consequences and their severity.

3. Risk Prioritization: Ranking the results to place more management effort on the highest risks.

Risk management then closes the loop by making decisions on how to deal with the risks assessed:

- Avoid the risk: Design the process to eliminate particular risks, minimize the risks, or change the nature of the risks to be faced.

- Control the risk: Institute procedures to control the process that minimize the consequences and severity of risk occurrence. This includes accepting some risk.

- Share the risk: Through contractual arrangements with suppliers, customers, constituents, or third parties (such as insurers), apportion some of the risk or risky activities to others and accepting the remainder.

There is always an amount of **residual risk** left over after all efforts have been made to avoid, control, or share the risk. If the residual risk is too high, then the task should not be done. If the residual risk is not too high, management may choose to accept this amount of risk in order to achieve objectives.

In addition to the residual risks left over from efforts of risk management, there are risks inherent in the management process known as **control risks**, or those risks associated with relying upon a control procedure, etc., that fails to accomplish its task. Both residual risk and control risk need to be explicitly dealt with in project management.

Major projects should be assessed by the project initiator and the functional or area management team. High risk factors should be examined for possible risk management action (avoid through redesign, additional controls, contractual arrangements, etc.). After proposed changes to the project plan are made, the project is again assessed, and management judgment is applied to test whether the change in risk assessment for the high risk factors is worth the extra costs (if any) of the risk management efforts. An additional assessment is recommended: that is the risk of not doing the project. *A comparison of this risk with the best (lowest risk) redesign of the project will give management information to make the decision whether to proceed or not.*

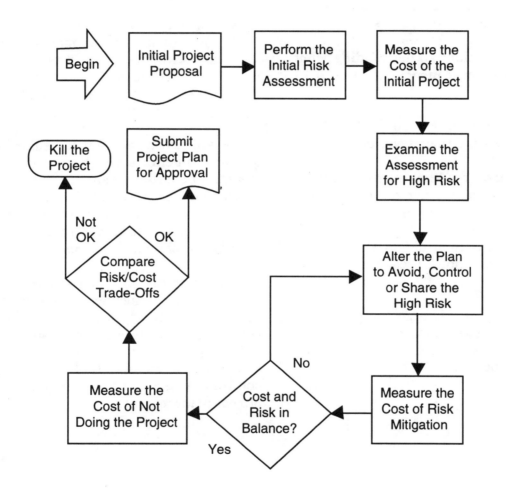

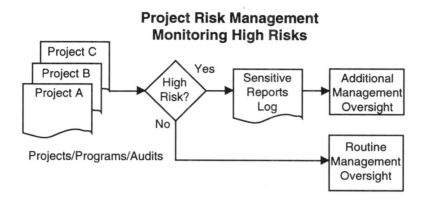

**Project Risk Management
Monitoring High Risks**

For ongoing business risk management, project management should use the information gained to enhance risk management techniques. Each of the organization's entities that uses risk assessment should establish a *Sensitive Projects* list of projects that are either high risk overall or those that may have high risk in certain key areas (whatever are the most sensitive areas for your organization). The list would vary in size, depending on the entity.

In addition, middle managers may want to assess or monitor their portfolio of lower level project managers' projects. These supervisory reviews compare relative risk assessments in order to provide more support to higher risk projects, either in terms of more personal management attention or in notifying functional support managers in the region of possible involvement in local projects. Sensitive projects should be monitored through regular reports and thorough review at regular staff meetings.

Risk management is the act of doing something with the information generated by the risk assessment. It is the necessary action step that uses all of the information provided to make efficient and effective decisions. Managers put assets at risk to achieve objectives. These decisions need to be supported by an efficient and effective business risk assessment and risk management process.

Project Risk Management: Self-Assessment Questionnaire

The questionnaire on the following pages may be reproduced and distributed to project management teams as an aid to assessing and managing risk.

Project Risk Management Self-Assessment

A	Risk Identification	Risk	Control Description or Action Plan
1.	Are risks identified on a regular basis throughout the project?	New risks, positive or negative, are not identified and addressed when necessary.	
2.	Does risk identification address both internal and external risks?	Not all risks are identified and addressed.	
3.	Are other planning outputs (work breakdown structure, cost estimates, etc.) used to identify risks?	Risk identification is incomplete.	
4.	Are historical information used to identify risks?	Risk identification is incomplete.	
5.	Are interviews with stakeholders held to identify risks not identified during the normal planning process?	Risk identification is incomplete.	
6.	Is flowcharting or equivalent used to understand the causes and effects of risk?	Proper risk response and control may not be effectively developed.	
7.	Are sources of risks, potential risk events, and risk symptoms identified and documented?	Proper risk response and control may not be effectively developed.	
8.	Do other processes take into consideration results from risk identification?	Improvements or changes to control risk are not made.	

Project Risk Management Self-Assessment

B	Risk Measurement Risk Prioritization	Risk	Control Description or Action Plan
1.	Does the measurement and prioritization process help determine which risk events warrant response?	Proper risk response and control may not be developed.	
2.	Are stakeholder risk tolerances considered in risk prioritization?	Risk measurement and prioritization may be inaccurate.	
3.	Are sources of risk, potential risk events, cost estimates, and activity duration estimates considered?	Risk measurement and prioritization may be inaccurate.	
4.	Are steps taken to ensure that the mathematical techniques used are appropriate and effective?	Methods used to measure risk may be unnecessary or inadequate.	
5.	Is expert judgment used when necessary?	Risk measurement is inaccurate.	
6.	Does risk prioritization result in a list of opportunities that need to be pursued and threats that need attention?	Proper risk response and control may not be developed.	
7.	Does the risk assessment process document the sources of risk and risk events that the project team consciously decided to accept/ignore and who made that decision?	No accountability for important decisions.	

Project Risk Management Self-Assessment

C	Risk Response Risk Management	Risk	Control Description or Action Plan
1.	Are steps taken to ensure that all outputs of the risk assessment process are used to develop risk response?	Responses to risk may be ineffective.	
2.	Is contingency planning done to determine the action steps to be taken if a risk event occurs?	Responses to risk may be ineffective.	
3.	Are alternative strategies considered to prevent risk events?	Steps to avoid or prevent unnecessary risk-taking are not identified.	
4.	Are procurement strategies and insurance considered for developing risk responses?	Steps to avoid or prevent unnecessary risk-taking are not identified.	
5.	Are procedures that will be used to manage risk throughout the project life cycle documented in the risk management plan?	The risk management plan may be incomplete and ineffective.	
6.	Do other processes take into consideration results from risk response development?	Improvements or changes to control risk are not made.	
7.	Are reserves established to mitigate cost and/or schedule risk?	Steps to adequately address risk are not taken.	
8.	Are contractual agreements entered into, when appropriate, in order to share, avoid or mitigate threats?	Steps to adequately address risk are not taken.	

Project Risk Management Self-Assessment

D	Risk Response Risk Management	Risk	Control Description or Action Plan
1.	Is the risk management plan used as a guide for risk response control?	Risk response control may not be in compliance with procedures.	
2.	Are steps taken to ensure that the project team recognizes when risk events occur?	Risk response control may fail.	
3.	Are additional risk assessments and risk responses part of risk response control?	New risks may not be identified and addressed.	
4.	Are necessary responses to risk events made, whether planned or unplanned?	Risk response control may fail.	
5.	Is the risk management plan updated when needed?	Risk management plan loses its applicability and/or effectiveness.	

SUGGESTED ANSWERS
TO EXERCISES

Note: The purpose of the exercises is to stimulate thinking about some aspect of business risk assessment. The suggested answers presented here are only examples and guides to facilitate understanding. There are many ways to answer each of these exercises, all of which are equally "correct."

Exercise 1: Using Risk Analysis in Decisions

Risk analysis is about making decisions with multiple alternatives under some degree of uncertainty as to the alternatives' outcomes.

1. Comment on the CEO's thinking process. Who else on the CEO's staff (or others) should provide input? What kind of input could that be?

    The CEO thought about risk assessment considering only external risks (market demand and interest rates) and consulted only with the CFO. There may have been other risks to consider that were internal or inherent in the process, such as the amount of disruption an office move normally generates. The CEO thought about this problem almost entirely alone. The CEO may have developed a broader and more thorough assessment if others had been brought into the thinking process. One obvious helper might be internal auditing — they might be able to verify key data and assumptions used in the decision as well as provide risk assessment expertise. Others that might be brought in could be a cross-section of people affected by the move to provide their views. The CEO went through the classic risk management options (diversify or avoid the risk, share or transfer the risk, and control or accept the risk), but the CEO needed a broader group to generate ideas about risk and solutions for managing that risk.

2. Is there a clear-cut decision to be made? Why or why not?

    There is a decision to be made, because the statement that the organization is outgrowing its space. Even postponing the decision (doing nothing now) is making a decision.

3. Do you see any additional risks or factors to be considered? Where might we look for additional concerns?

    In addition to the risk of the office move creating disruption, there may be other risks that come from within the process itself. Examine the major assets in the headquarters building, including its present location. There may be political reasons for expanding the location instead of relocating to another community or neighborhood. The present location may be ideal for many of the lower paid employees to use public transportation, and the new location may not have that access. Certain infrastructure (computers, telecommunications) may create complexities if they are to be moved.

Exercise 2: Three-Way Risk Identification

Risk cannot be effectively managed until it is identified. Most of us use an intuitive approach to risk identification — from experience and common sense we can name the most important risks. Sometimes this is not enough, especially when attempting to assess new or unfamiliar operations. To understand thoroughly the sources of risk in those cases, we suggest a three-way approach to risk identification.

Your team has been asked to come up with a risk-based branch audit manual, so that the audits can be more efficient and effective. As part of this effort, your group must identify the major sources of risk for the standard branch audit in the following format:

Risk Profile: Branch Banking

Exposure Analysis:

Risk Source	Why?
1. Cash and securities	Attractive asset needs protection
2. Loan portfolio	Major revenue stream
3. Customer-focused employees	Source of new/continuing customers
4. Reputation	Key asset for competition
5. Customer data	Private information needs protection

Environmental Analysis:

Risk Source	Why?
1. Competitors	Changes in acquisition patterns
2. Customers	Changes in requirements/needs
3. Regulation	Changes in banking rules to allow additional competition sources or create additional expenses

Threat Scenarios:

Risk Source	Why?
1. Employee fraud	Cash handling
2. Natural disaster	Disrupt operations
3. Major utility failure (power/telecom)	Disrupt operations

Exercise 3: Operational Risk Identification

Sometimes the risks in operational auditing issues (efficient and effective operations) are more difficult to handle than compliance or financial audits.

Management has asked your advice about the risks in establishing a recycling program. In your team, identify the risks in the above recycling scheme. Use this format:

Risk Profile: Operational Audit

Exposure Analysis:

Risk Source	Why?
Customer private data	Could be stolen by recycler
Reputation	(Positive) seen as "green"

Environmental Analysis:

Risk Source	Why?
Suppliers	Changes in rates from city and recyclers may affect costs

Threat Scenarios:

Risk Source	Why?
Fraud	Customer data could be sold

Bottom Line: The revenue potential of 2.5 tons of white paper per month is $100 and cost savings from the city garbage collection is $290 for a total potential of $390. Considering the dangers of exposing customer private information and the unknown hidden costs of separating the trash for recycling, it does not appear to be a good idea.

Exercise 4: Measuring and Classifying Risk

There are a number of approaches to measuring risk. For the annual plan or for homogeneous audit units (plants, branches, field offices, etc.), risk factors work well. For individual audits, other methods such as normative tables are more effective.

In your teams:

Given the four categories of risk, the controls usually relied upon, the prior audit findings, the environment, and the operating data:

1. Develop a method for measuring and classifying these four risks into Low, Medium, or High Risk areas. Be able to justify your reasons for the classification. Use the format that follows.

2. Given a budget of 40 hours of fieldwork, how would you allocate your time among these four areas?

Begin by building a "yardstick" — what the characteristics of risk levels look like in relation to the operations of the bank. Define the risk characteristics based on various levels of known sources of risk:

Risk Level	Description of Characteristics
High Risk	Lack of dual custody, separation of duties, or adequate supervision. Difficult-to-determine values, or values are self-assessed and subjectively represented. Values are large in comparison with total revenue. Values can fluctuate widely. Processes are manual and may require a great deal of judgment. Processes are subject to internal control override.
Medium Risk	Some weaknesses noted in custody, duties, or supervision. Values can be verified independently with some effort. Values are moderate in comparison with total revenue. Values fluctuate within reasonable ranges. Processes are computerized but also have a lot of special processes or exceptions. Processes depend heavily on internal control.
Low Risk	Strong controls over custody and supervision of employees. Values are well-documented, or trades are published on open markets. Values are small and stable (or predictable). Processes are highly automated and routine. Internal controls are highly redundant.

National Bank Northeast Branch Risk Classification

A. | **Risk** | **Classification** | **Why?**

1. Loans to insiders — Medium

Process of reporting is manual and subject to error; loans are secured, and total value is 0.2% of all property loans. Collateral values predictable but declining. Automated repayment.

2. Collateral verification — Medium

Values are high compared to total assets. Documentation of values are independently derived. Manual process of verification.

3. Collateral maintenance — High

Values are high compared to total assets. Manual verification process. Highly dependent on controls, and the process can be overridden or ignored.

4. Repayments — Low

Process is highly automated and routine. Past history of defaults are very low (0.8%). Individual transaction values are very small (each).

B. **Budget Allocation in Hours:** **Reasons:**

1. **Insider Loans:** **10** — Average Risk (Medium) = 40/4 = 10

2. **Collateral Verification:** **10** — Average Risk (Medium) = 40/4 = 10

3. **Collateral Maintenance:** **15** — Higher Risk should get a premium

4. **Repayments:** **5** — Lower Risk should get less review.

Any sort of distribution that puts more effort where there is more risk and less effort where there is less risk demonstrates an understanding of the point of this part of the exercise. With everything being the same (Medium Risk), the average equates to 10 hours over each of the four areas. High risk should be more (15 hours in this example) and Low Risk less (five hours).

Exercise 5: Risk Assessment Case Study – Part I

This is an exercise in three parts:
- Part I: Risk Identification
- Part II: Develop Risk Matrix
- Part II: Evaluate the Strength and Weaknesses in Control

Part I asks the participants to use brainstorming and multi-voting to develop a list of threats to the reliability and security of the data center and pare the list down to the eight most significant threats.

Data Center Risk Identification

Threats	Why?
1. **Cooling system mechanical failure**	Excessive heat will damage the CPU
2. **Natural disaster (flood, etc.)**	Basement location is vulnerable to flooding
3. **Extensive power failure**	System unavailable to users
4. **Fire (and fire suppression system)**	Fire and Halon system can render the system unavailable for some time
5. **Data corruption**	Data becomes unavailable or must be recreated at great expense
6. **Data backup failure**	Data becomes unavailable or must be recreated at great expense
7. **Hackers/Intentional Threats**	Data corruption or system unavailable
8. **Key component failure**	Data corruption or system unavailable

Other Threats (Optional):

9. **Physical sabotage**

10. **Telecom network failure**

11. **Strike by employees**

12. **Loss of skilled employees**

13. **Etc.**

Exercise 5: Risk Assessment Case Study – Part II

To build a risk matrix requires an identification of risks (Part I) and the components of the system (Part II):

Data Center Component Identification

Important Component	Why?
1. Hardware (including telecom network)	Main system physical components
2. Software	Operating systems and data applications
3. HVAC and Power	Main physical support components
4. Physical Protection	System of protective elements that are key parts to the control system
5. People	System requires system operators
6. Policies and Procedures	Directs the people to tasks that need to be done and the sequence of the tasks

(Only 6 fit on the diagram)

Other Important Components (Optional):

You could separately identify some topics from some of the groupings such as telecom networks, preventative maintenance, backup & recovery system, UPS, etc.

Exercise 5: Risk Assessment Case Study – Part III

The matrix elements will depend upon what was selected as risks in Part I and components in Part II. Based on our previous suggested answers, the following matrix/table could emerge:

If the two axes are sorted so that:
1. The high risks are on the left of the top axis and low risk on the right, and
2. The most important components are on the top of the left axis and the least important on the bottom, then

The upper left quadrant becomes the HIGH RISK AREA and the lower right quadrant becomes the LOW RISK AREA. If the auditor makes a valuation of controls for the matrix by assigning each cell a letter (S = Strong controls, W = Weak controls, Blank = Unknown or Moderate), a sense of the level of testing that will be necessary can be recorded in the matrix – in addition to the relative risks involved.

Final Risk Matrix

	Cooling System Mechanical Failure	Natural Disaster, Flood, etc.	Extensive Power Failure	Fire (and fire suppression system)	Data Corruption	Data Backup Failure	Hackers/ Intentional Threats	Key Component Failure
Hardware								
Software								
HVAC and Power								
Physical Protection								
People								
Policies and Procedures								

GLOSSARY

Absolute Risk: Pure risk without the mitigating effects of **Internal Controls** (see also **Managed Risk**).

Analytic Hierarchy Process (AHP): A mathematical process involving matrices that produces a **Ranking** through **Pair-Wise Comparison** voting of competing alternatives and different criteria.

Audit: An examination or review that compares "what is" with "what should be" and provides **Feedback** for corrective action.

Audit Plan: The annual plan of audits to be accomplished.

Audit Program: The plan of the audit of a particular topic, subject, project, department, process, or function.

Audit Universe: The sum of all **Auditable Units** for an organization.

Auditable Unit: Any particular topic, subject, project, department, process, or function that is worthy of an audit.

Bias: In models, the tendency to favor one set of outcomes regardless of the variability of the inputs.

Cadbury: A system of internal controls or **Control Framework** defined by the Cadbury Commission (UK).

CoActive Auditing: An approach to auditing that depends on **Collaborative Techniques**, such as involving the audit customer in the audit process.

CoCo: A system of internal controls or **Control Framework** defined by the Canadian Criteria of Control Committee of the CICA.

Collaborative Techniques: In risk assessment, a range of methods to incorporate multiple assessments, estimations, and judgments about risk into a single consensus. See **CoActive Auditing** and **Delphi Technique**.

Confidence Dispersion: The measure of uncertainty about an estimate. In auditing, it has been used as a measure of uncertainty about **Control Risk** due to the passage of time between audits. The longer the time, the greater the risk (or greater dispersion of confidence in control effectiveness).

Consensus: General agreement in principle. Does not imply total agreement or unanimous assent.

Consequences: The outcomes of the decisions, events, or processes.

Control: See **Internal Control**.

Control Framework: A recognized system of control categories that covers all internal controls expected in an organization. Control frameworks include **COSO**, **CoCo**, **Cadbury**, and the like.

Control and Risk Self-Assessment: Abbreviated **CRSA**. See **Control Self-Assessment**.

Control Risk: The tendency of the **Internal Control** system to lose effectiveness over time and to expose, or fail to prevent exposure of, the assets under control.

Control Self-Assessment: Abbreviated **CSA**. A class of techniques used in an audit or in place of an audit to assess risk and control strength and weaknesses against a **Control Framework**. The "self" assessment refers to the involvement of management and staff in the assessment process, often facilitated by internal auditors.

Controls Evaluation Tables: A **Risk Analysis** technique that focuses on the strengths of **Internal Controls** to mitigate the risks. The analysis is performed using a tabular representation of the risks vs. controls and a measure of the control strength.

COSO: A system of internal controls or **Control Framework** defined by the Committee of Sponsoring Organizations of the Treadway Commission (USA).

Criteria: Requirements.

CRSA: See **Control and Risk Assessment**.

CSA: See **Control Self-Assessment**.

Data Flow Diagrams: A graphical depiction of the major flows of data and how these flows are linked. Used in place of **Flow Charting**. Useful in **Risk Identification** and **Risk Scenarios** to determine the points of greatest **Exposure**.

Delphi Technique: A **Collaborative Technique** involving independent analysis and voting by experts given perfect **Feedback** as to how their judgment matches that of the remainder of the group as a whole.

Detection Risk: A concept from public accounting. See AICPA *SAS No. 47*, 1983). The **Probability** that an incorrect **Audit** conclusion will be drawn from the results of the examination.

Direct Assignment: The assignment of preference weights to risk factors by estimation. See also **Pair-Wise Comparison**.

Direct Estimation: Polite term for guessing or "educated" guessing.

Event Trees: A method of **Risk Identification** and **Consequence** evaluation where all possible subsequent events are evaluated for their **Risk**. Used in risk scenarios.

Expected Value Approach: The evaluation of **Risk** based on the dollar variation that results as a **Consequence** to the risky events.

Exposure: The susceptibility to loss, perception of **Risk**, or a **Threat** to an asset or asset-producing process, usually quantified in dollars. An exposure is the total dollars at risk without regard to the probability of a negative event. A measure of importance.

Fault Trees: A method of **Risk Identification** and **Risk Scenario** building where the end result of an event is traced backwards to all possible causes.

Feedback: In systems and models, the flow of information about the present condition of variables to the originator or source for the purposes of monitoring the achievement of objectives.

Flow Chart: A graphical depiction of the major tasks and activities in a function and how they are linked. Useful in **Risk Identification** and **Risk Scenarios** to determine the points of greatest **Exposure**.

Inherent Risk: The risk found in the environment and in human activities that is part of existence.

Internal Control: All the means, tangible and intangible that can be employed or used to ensure that established objectives are met.

Long Term: The planning or **Time Horizon** that deals with events beyond the **Short Term** and **Mid Term**, typically from two to 20 years, though most often two to five or seven years.

LRAM: The Livermore Risk Analysis Methodology developed by Charles Cresson Wood using both control failure and **Vulnerability Analysis** to generate **Risk Scenarios**.

Macro Risk Assessment: The categorization and assessment of **Auditable Units** into an overall plan of audits for the organization (**Audit Plan**).

Managed Risk: The risks and consequences after the application of **Internal Control** (see also **Absolute Risk**).

Matrix Approach: In **Risk Assessment**, an approach that matches system components with risks, threats or controls with the object of measuring and examining the combinations of the two axes.

Micro Risk Assessment: The categorization and assessment of the functions, tasks, positions, processes, subsystems and subunits of an **Auditable Unit** for the purposes of planning the audit of that unit (**Audit Program**).

Mid Term: The planning or **Time Horizon** that deals with events in the middle period between **Short Term** and **Long Term**, typically beyond the current year and for one or two years further.

Mission Analysis: A technique that addresses **Audit Program** development by examining a process from many different approaches that can fulfill the function's mission: categorizing outcomes, geography served, compliance issues and the like.

Multidimensional Approach: An approach to **Risk Assessment** that views **Risk** and **Opportunity** through various **Time Horizons** or dimensions as manifestations of the same uncertainty. This approach best approximates senior management's strategic planning.

Opportunity: An uncertain event with a positive probable **Consequence**. Related to **Risk**.

Pair-Wise Comparison: The assignment of preference weights to **Risk Factors** and/or system components using a voting technique that compares all possible pairs of choices. See also **Direct Assignment** and **Analytic Hierarchy Process (AHP)**.

Paradigm: A "view" of how things work in the world. In **Risk Scenarios** or **Threat Scenarios**, paradigms are used to set the basic rules of how the world works so that the solutions can be set within some boundaries.

Pervasive Risk: The type of risk found throughout the environment. The focus is on the environment of the business activity instead of the activity itself. Think of it as the "Corporate Culture."

Planning Risk: The risk that the planning process is flawed. In **Risk Assessment**, it is the risk that the assessment process is inappropriate or improperly implemented.

Portfolio Risk: In **Risk Analysis**, it is the risk that a particular combination of projects, assets, units or whatever is in the portfolio will fail to meet the overall objectives of the portfolio due to poor balance of risks within the portfolio.

Probability: A measure (expressed as a percentage or ratio) of estimation.

Process Failure Risk Model: A specialized **Risk Model** that makes use of multiple **Risk Scenarios** and **Exposure** assessments as well as feedback loops to continuously update scenarios and exposures to changes in the process.

Ranking: The process of establishing the order or priority.

Risk: A measure of uncertainty. In the business process, the uncertainty is about the achievement of organizational objectives. May involve positive or negative **Consequences**, although most positive risks are known as **Opportunities** and negative risks are called simply risks.

Risk Analysis: The identification of risk, the measurement of risk, and the process of prioritizing risks or selecting alternatives based on risk.

Risk Assessment: The identification of risk, the measurement of risk, and the process of prioritizing risks.

Risk Classification: The categorization of risk, typically into High, Medium, Low and intermediate values.

Risk Evaluation: See **Risk Measurement**.

Risk Factors: Measurable or observable manifestations or characteristics of a process that either indicates the presence of **Risk** or tends to increase **Exposure**.

Risk Identification: The method of recognizing possible **Threats** and **Opportunities**.

Risk Management: A branch of management that deals with the **Consequences** of risk. Quite often this function handles the supervision of insurance policies.

Risk Measurement: The evaluation of the magnitude of risk.

Risk Model: A mathematical, graphical or verbal description of risk for a particular environment and set of activities within that environment. Useful in **Risk Assessment** for consistency, training and documentation of the assessment.

Risk Prioritization: The relation of acceptable levels of risks among alternatives. See also **Risk Ranking**.

Risk Ranking: The ordinal or cardinal rank prioritization of the risks in various alternatives, projects, or units.

Risk Response: The actions taken to manage risk.

Risk Scenarios: A method of identifying and classifying risks through creative application of **Probabilistic** events and their **Consequences**. Typically a brainstorming or other creative technique is used to stimulate "what might happen." See also **Threat Scenarios**.

Robust: Related to **Risk Models**, robustness is a measure of a model's strength in handling data and data errors without model failure.

SAS No. 47: "Statement on Audit Risk and Materiality." A reference for U.S. public accountants on **Risk Assessment** in their work.

SAS No. 55: "Consideration of the Internal Control Structure in a Financial Statement Audit." Expands and builds on *SAS No. 47* defining the kinds of risk to be accounted for in the public accountant's work.

Short Term: The planning or **Time Horizon** that deals with events within the current cycle or accounting period (typically one year, occasionally two years).

SIAS No. 9: "Risk Assessment." A reference for the internal audit profession on **Macro Risk Assessment** to guide their work.

SISAS No. 5: "Risk Assessment." A reference for the internal information systems audit profession on **Risk Assessment** to guide their work.

Specific Risk: The type of risk that is found in specific activities. The level of this risk is expected to vary from activity to activity, even though all activities may have it.

Strategic Risk/Opportunity Curve: A model developed by David McNamee to express the changing nature of the **Consequences** of negative **Risk** and positive **Opportunity** over multiple **Time Horizons**.

SWAT: Strengths/Weaknesses Analysis Technique. Used in **Control Self-Assessment** and **Risk Scenarios** concerning the strengths and weaknesses of **Internal Control**. Recognizes that too strong is as important as too weak, as both induce variability in the achievement of organizational objectives.

Threat: A combination of the **Risk**, the **Consequence** of that risk, and the likelihood that the negative event will take place. Often used in analysis in place of **Risk**.

Threat Matrix: A matrix of **Threats** and usually system components or system elements (tasks, functions, hardware, processes, software, people, etc.) for purposes of measuring and estimating the **Consequences** or the **Internal Control** of various combinations.

Threat Scenarios: Similar to **Risk Scenarios**, except the focus is on the negative **Consequences** of uncertain events.

Time Horizons: Planning horizons used in **Risk Scenarios** and strategic planning to represent different time periods. Often: **Short Term**, **Mid Term** and **Long Term**.

Uncertainty: A condition where the outcome can only be estimated.

Vulnerability Analysis: Introduced by William Perry, includes the **Expected Value Approach** with the added dimension of **Time Horizons**.

BIBLIOGRAPHY

Books and Videos

ACEA/The Institute of Engineers, Australia, *Dealing with Risk*, March 1993.

American Institute of Certified Public Accountants, *Statement on Auditing Standards No. 47* "Audit Risk and Materiality" (NY: AICPA, 1983).

American Institute of Certified Public Accountants, *Statement on Auditing Standards No. 55* "Consideration of the Internal Control Structure in a Financial Statement Audit" (NY: AICPA, 1988).

Arthur Andersen & Co., *Evaluation of Internal Controls* (St. Charles, IL: Arthur Andersen & Co., 1987).

Australian Department of Administrative Services, *Managing Risk in Procurement Handbook* (Australian Government Publishing Service, 1996).

Australian Management Advisory Board, *Managing Risk* (Exposure Draft), July 1995.

Barrett, Michael J, *Risk Analysis Symposium* (Video and Discussion Leader's Guide) (Altamonte Springs, FL: The Institute of Internal Auditors, 1988).

Boritz, J. Efrim, *Planning for the Internal Audit Function* (Altamonte Springs, FL: The Institute of Internal Auditors Research Foundation, 1983).

Comptroller of the Currency, *Large Bank Supervision* (Risk Assessment), December 1995.

Comptroller General of the United States, *Government Auditing Standards (revised)*, (Washington, DC: U.S. Government Printing Office, 1994).

Courtemanche, Gil, *The New Internal Auditing* (NY: John Wiley & Sons, 1986).

Davis, Keagle W. and William E. Perry, *Auditing Computer Applications* (NY: John Wiley & Sons, 1982).

Delbecq, Andre L., Andrew Van de Ven, and David H. Gustafson, *Group Techniques for Program Planning* (Glenview, IL: Scott Foresman, 1975).

EDP Auditors Foundation, *Statement on Information Systems Auditing Standards No. 5* "Performance of Work: The Use of Risk Analysis in Audit Planning" (Carol Stream, IL: EDPAF, 1992).

FitzGerald, Jerry and Ardra F., *Designing Controls in Computerized Systems 2nd ed.* (Redwood City, CA: Jerry FitzGerald & Associates, 1990).

Gallegos, Frederick, Dana R. Richardson, and A. Faye Borthick, *Audit and Control of Information Systems* (Cincinnati, OH: South-Western Publishing Co., 1987).

Financial Executives Institute, *COSO Self-Assessment Framework* (Software) (Altamonte Springs, FL: IIA (407-830-7600 X1), 1994).

Hertz, David B. and Howard Thomas, *Practical Risk Analysis* (NY: John Wiley & Sons, 1984).

Hertz, David B. and Howard Thomas, *Risk Analysis and Its Applications* (NY: John Wiley & Sons, 1983).

The Institute of Internal Auditors, *Codification of Standards for the Professional Practice of Internal Auditing* (Altamonte Springs, FL: The Institute of Internal Auditors, 1995).

The Institute of Internal Auditors, *Statement on Internal Auditing Standards No. 9 "Risk Assessment"* (Altamonte Springs, FL: The Institute of Internal Auditors, 1992).

Keeney, Ralph L. and Howard Raiffa, *Decisions with Multiple Objectives: Preferences and Tradeoffs* (NY: John Wiley & Sons, 1976).

Kendall, M.G., *Rank Correlation Methods 2nd ed.* (NY: Hafner, 1955).

Mair, William C., Donald R. Wood, and Keagle W. Davis, *Computer Control and Audit Rev. ed.* (Altamonte Springs, FL: The Institute of Internal Auditors, 1978).

Mautz, R. K. and James Winjum, *Criteria for Management Control Systems* (NY: Financial Executives Research Foundation, 1981).

McNamee, David W., *Assessing Risk* (Altamonte Springs, FL: The Institute of Internal Auditors, 1996).

McNamee, David W., *Assessing Risk: A Better Way to Audit* (Seminar) (Altamonte Springs, FL: The Institute of Internal Auditors, 1995).

McNamee, David W. and Frances A., *Audit Excellence: Best Practices and Total Quality Management* (Video and Workbook) (Altamonte Springs, FL: The Institute of Internal Auditors, 1993).

McNamee, David W., *Audit Excellence: Best Practices and TQM* (Walnut Creek, CA: Management Control Concepts, 1992).

McNamee, David W., *Audit Risk Assessment: Text and Seminar Workbook* (Walnut Creek, A: Management Control Concepts, 1996).

McNamee, David W., *Facilitated Self Assessment* (Walnut Creek, CA: Management Control Concepts, 1995).

McNamee, David W., *Risk Assessment in the 90s* (Walnut Creek, CA: Management Control Concepts, 1993).

Office of the Auditor General of Canada, *Internal Auditing in a Changing Management Culture* (Office of the Auditor General of Canada, Ottawa, ON: 1992).

Patton, James M., John H. Evans III, and Barry L. Lewis, *A Framework for Evaluating Internal Audit Risk* (Altamonte Springs, FL: The Institute of Internal Auditors, 1983).

Perry, Davis and McNamee, *Handbook for Internal Auditors* (Release 15) (New York, NY: Matthew Bender & Co., 1995).

Sawyer, Lawrence B. and Glenn E. Sumners, *Sawyer's Internal Auditing 3rd ed.* (Altamonte Springs, FL: The Institute of Internal Auditors, 1988).

Sherer, Susan A., *Software Failure Risk: Measurement and Management* (NY: Plenum Press, 1992).

Tuck, Richard, *An Interview with Larry Harrington of LTV Corp.* (Video) (Richmond, CA: Lander International, 1992).

Willborn, Walter, *Audit Standards: A Comparative Analysis (Second Edition)* (Milwaukee, WI: ASQC Quality Press, 1993).

Journal Articles

Armstrong, Ronald D., Wade D. Cook and Lawrence M. Seiford, "Priority Ranking and Consensus Formation: The Case of Ties," *Management Science*, Vol. 28, No. 6, June 1982.

Barrett, M. J., "Allocating Resources with Strength/Weakness Analysis," *Internal Auditor*, June 1986.

Blair, W. P., "Auditing on the Leading Edge: The Risk Catalyst," *Internal Audit Review* (South Africa), July 1993.

Caster, Paul, "An Analysis of Techniques for Assessing Risk," *The EDP Auditor Journal*, Vol. III, 1987.

Cerullo, Michael J. and Fred A. Shelton, "Quantitative Evaluation: A New Way to Measure Computer Security," *CA Magazine*, October 1980.

Colbert, Janet, "Use the Concept of Inherent Risk — It Helps!," *Internal Auditor*, April 1987.

Cook, Wade D. and Lawrence M. Seiford, "On the Borda-Kendall Consensus Method for Priority Ranking Problems," *Management Science*, Vol. 28, No. 6, June 1982.

Cottrell, David M., et al., *Continuous Improvement at Clorox, Internal Auditor*, February 1995.

Davidson, Barco D., "A Risk Assessment Approach to Systems Development Auditing," *The EDP Auditor Journal*, Vol. II 1987.

EDPACS, "Introducing CRAMM," *EDPACS*, February 1994.

Erickson, John, "Integrated Risk Assessment," *IS Audit and Control Journal*, Vol. VI, 1995.

Evens, Mark, "Data Flow Risk Analysis" *Internal Auditing* (U.K.), May 1991, reprinted in *AUDIT NEWZ* (N.Z.), March 1993.

Farrell, Thomas F., "Quality Controls — Business Controls: Two Sides of the Same Issue," *The Business Control Newsletter*, September-October 1992

FitzGerald, Jerry, "Developing and Ranking Threat Scenarios," *EDPACS*, August 1978.

Gray, O. Ronald, "Audit Project Evaluation Methodology," *Internal Auditor*, June 1983.

Haig, Nancy, "How to Perform a Risk Assessment in Healthcare Internal Audit," *New Perspectives in Healthcare Auditing*, April 1996.

Haskins, Mark E. and Robert L. Henarie, "Attributes and Audit Impact of Client's Control Environment," *The CPA Journal*, July 1985.

Hayward, James, "Risk Assessment," *Internal Auditing* (UK), September 1995.

Hemaida, Ramadan, "A Practical Model to Audit Risk Assessment in a Health-Care Setting," *Managerial Auditing Journal*, Vol. 10 No. 5 (1995).

Hunton, James E. and Jesse D. Beeler, "Targeting Potential Audit Risk Areas on Radar Graphs," *IS Audit & Control Journal*, Vol. IV, 1995.

Hyde, Gerald E., "Risk Analysis and Program Development," *Internal Auditor*, June 1986.

The Institute of Internal Auditors, "Statement of Responsibilities of Internal Auditing," (Rev.), IIA, 1990.

Juarez, Antonio, "Risk Assessment in State Government," IIA Austin (Texas) Chapter Research Project, manuscript, May 1993.

Kanter, Howard K., John E. McEnroe, and Mary C. Kyes, "Developing and Installing an Audit Risk Model," *Internal Auditor*, December 1990.

McClave, Norman, "Approaches to Managing Risk," *Bank Management*, March/April 1996.

McNamee, David W., "Assessing Risk Assessment," *New Perspectives on Healthcare Auditing*, April 1996.

McNamee, David W., "Developing an IS Risk Assessment Process," *IS Audit & Control Journal*, Volume III, 1996.

McNamee, David W., "How to Achieve Goals with the Right Mix of Plans," *Bankers Journal Malaysia*, Number 91, October-November 1995.

McNamee, David W., "A New Approach to Business Risk," *Business Control Magazine*, June 1994.

McNamee, David W., and Thomas S., "Breakpoint," *Internal Auditor*, December 1992.

Mohr, Joseph H. and Patrick Ruckh, "Risk Analysis of Software Systems," in *EDP Auditing* (Pennsauken, NJ: Auerbach Publishers, Inc., 1985).

Mroch, Chris A., "Practical Audit-risk Analysis," *Internal Auditor*, August 1987.

Perry, William E., "Auditing the Data Center: An Introduction," in *EDP Auditing* (Pennsauken, NJ: Auerbach Publishers, Inc., 1985).

Roberts, Ray and Steven T. Giorgione, "Comparison Risk Ranking Applications," *Journal of Accountancy*, May 1995.

Ross, Steven J., "Risk Analysis Environments," *The EDP Auditor Journal*, Vol. II 1987.

Saaty, Thomas L., "A Scaling Method for Priorities in Hierarchical Structures," *Journal of Mathematical Psychology*, June 1977.

Siers, Howard L. and Joanne K. Blyskal, "Risk Management of the Internal Audit Function," *Management Accounting*, February 1987.

Sittenfield, Itamar, "Audit Planning with the Grid Model," *Internal Auditor*, February 1991.

Steele, J. Douglas, "Matching Audit Objectives with Management Goals," *Internal Auditor*, June 1993.

Storslee, M. D. and D. W. Breckel, "The PDQ Prioritizer," *Internal Auditor*, April 1984.

Thompson, George T., "Risk Assessment and the Audit Function," *Internal Audit Advisor*, Vol. 1 No. 8, February 1986.

Thompson, James H. and Janet L. Colbert, "How to Incorporate Inherent Risk into Statistical Sampling in Auditing," *The EDP Auditor Journal*, Vol. I, 1991.

Walz, Anthony P., "An Integrated Risk Model," *Internal Auditor*, April 1991.

Zeigenfuss, Douglas E., "The State of the Art in Internal Auditing Risk Assessment Techniques," *Managerial Auditing Journal*, Vol. 10 No. 4 (1995).